DOG ~~Training~~

TEACHING

Surviving a Puppy
Without Losing Your Mind

A Teaching Book
By
Jane Young
www.foxfielddogtraining.com

On the cover:

Peter and Sue's Seastar's Northern Penny,
a Jasmine/Mensa pup. Photo by Kaila Bird

Credits:

Edited by Rae O'Leary
Designed by Bryan Young
Photographs by Bryan Young

Website:
www.foxfielddogtraining.com

This book is dedicated to Woody, who, in his short life, taught me the difference between training and teaching.

Table of Contents

Chapter 1

So, You Got a Puppy. Now What?

Twelve week old Riley with his family.

Well, the deed is done. The kids finally convinced you to get a puppy. Or maybe the kids all left home and you only have yourself to blame. Whatever be the details, here he is: an adorable, furry, bright-eyed torna-do of energy. So you never knew that tornadoes pee every ten seconds, no matter where they are? So you never knew that tornadoes chew on anything that fits into their needle-filled mouths? I want to welcome you to my world and that of all dog lovers. Now let's decide how to go about taming this wild beast and keep everyone and everything safe.

Establish Your Relationship With Your Puppy

Believe it or not, this whole puppy raising thing is all about the relationship you establish. I would like to convince you to banish the words 'alpha' and 'pack leader' from your doggie vocabulary. Oh, ya, I know: you read on the internet or heard on TV you must establish yourself as the alpha leader of your pack. Let me tell you that packs are for wolves and boy scouts. Dogs are NOT pack animals. Gasp!!! Nope, they're not. You know what they are? They are scavengers. Yup, they are seagulls with fur. If you want to know more about this, I recommend <u>Dogs: Their Ecology, Evolution and Behavior</u> by Ray and Lorna Coppinger.

Thinking of your puppy as a future pack member, who must be dominated, controlled and shown his proper place is not even close to how you want to think and feel about that little bundle of skunk-breathed energy. That puppy is your pet, your buddy, your walking partner, maybe even your sleeping companion. You don't need to dominate. You need to educate. A puppy is a blank slate, a sponge and putty in your hands. Instead of alpha, think of yourself as a teacher. You will be teaching your puppy how to live with you, how to follow your house rules, and how to be a good member of your family and community.

Choose a Teaching Philosophy

Woody: Ch Sagewood's Icon of Foxfield RE UD CGC WC ThD
VC. Photo by Barry Young

There are about as many dog training philosophies as there are dog trainers, plus one. Unfortunately, they all disagree and they all think they are right and everyone else is wrong. Well, it is really pretty simple: they will all train your puppy. Any method, no matter how kind or how cruel or how quick or how tedious, will train a dog if it is followed consistently. All you need to decide is which method to use. This quickly boils down to a choice in philosophy. Do you want to TRAIN with pain, fear, and domination? Or, would you rather TEACH. Do you want to harshly punish your pup for doing what is wrong, or would you rather teach him how to do what is right? The two basic choices, as I see it, are to harshly punish what is wrong or to teach and reward what is right. Combine the two, you ask? The reason I don't use this approach is that harsh punishment-based training is effective but can produce a cautious, timid attitude in the dog. The reward-based method, on the other hand, produces a creative, gleeful dog who is willing to take a risk since the payoff may be large. For him, painful or scary punishment is non-existent. I find combining the two does not give you the best of both, but rather a dog whose approach to learning is tentative since he doesn't know if he will be painfully punished or generously rewarded.

Many of us so-called positive trainers came from a punishment foundation. I have used my share of prong collars and slip (a nice word for choke) chains, and even the dreaded electric collar. I was in the midst of all of this when my beloved not-yet-four-year-old Nova Scotia Duck Tolling Retriever, Woody, became ill and was diagnosed with Severe Chronic Fibrosing Hepatitis with an inflammatory response. That is the scientific way of saying "he has less than a month to live". Well, after a week in the hospital and several thousand dollars later, he didn't die. He not only didn't die, he started to get better. I got really good at managing a chart full of daily meds and hiding pills in chicken breast, and he paid me back by slowly recovering, day by day, until he could return to daily walks in the woods and then to competition training.

In competition work I had been using harsh corrections to get the behaviors I wanted from Woody. Even though Woody was the type of dog that didn't really object, his illness made me see that I no longer wanted to use those methods. Life, particularly that of dogs, is too short to include pain and fear delivered by the human teacher. I vowed to Woody and to myself, before we ventured back into those dog schools, he would never, ever again be harshly corrected, if he promised to live. I would become what I came to learn was called a "cross-over" trainer, going from correction training to clicker training. I see it more simply: I crossed over from being cross to being kind. I would no longer use pain or fear to get a green qualifying ribbon the dog didn't even know he had earned! We walked back into the dog training ring and Woody finished five competition titles, many with placement level scores. Far more importantly, every morning he walked three miles a day with me and my other Toller, Foxy, and we watched the sun come through the tree branches while the early mist lifted off the lake where we are blessed to live. He gave me goodbye kisses when I left for work and ran through the doggy door to "wave" to me as I walked to the car from the house. He greeted me when I returned home and settled down with me each night.

That dog lived another six years rather than the month predicted. Those six years changed me forever. I learned that I could teach with kindness and praise and fix errors in a pain free way. I am the teacher I am today because of that dog. He will never leave my heart.

Manage Before You Teach

If you have decided to use a positive approach to teaching your puppy what is right, rather than harshly punishing him for what is wrong, all you need is a buckle collar, a four or six foot leash, some soft, tasty cookies (food reward) and a clicker. But, let's face it, teaching a tornado to be a well behaved pup will take time. You need some immediate relief from those spells of puppy crazies when you end up with shredded hem-lines, scratched arms and legs, and a pee-stained living room rug. This

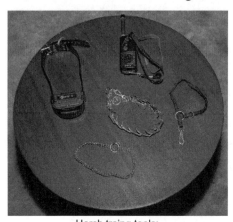

Harsh traing tools:
Choke chain, electric collar, prong collar and fabric choke.

Positive teaching must-haves:
Clicker, leash, cookies and buckle collar.

immediate relief comes, not in the form of teaching, but through manage-ment. Your tools for this are a crate, that same four to six foot leash, baby gates, an X-pen and a bottle of chewing deterrent such as Bitter Apple brand, Chew Not brand or one of many others on the market available online or at local pet stores.

The crate is to be used as your pup's happy place, a haven to which he can escape when his humans have reached their tolerance level. How to actually turn a simple crate into a haven is covered in the chapter on house training. You have probably been told that the crate is not to be used for punishment. I agree, unless you call a time-out a form of pun-ishment, which I don't. Time-out is time-out, nothing more. It is a well-de-served break for puppy and owner alike. Placing a pup in a cookie strewn crate, quietly closing the door and then going about your routine is not punishment.

Along similar lines, the leash can be used to stop the mania. When the pup is running around the kitchen as fast as he can, bouncing off walls like a racket ball, simply attach a leash to his buckle collar, drop the leash on the floor and step on the leash with the ball of one foot. Once you have become a human tether, quietly bend down and stroke the pup while you softly whisper sweet nothings to him. If he struggles to get free or bites at your hands, stand up but do not remove your foot from the leash. When he calms, repeat the praise. Attach some sort of 'Settle' word to his calm behavior so you can eventually ask for it with a verbal cue.

Settle with a foot on the leash.

Some puppies have trouble settling when your foot is on the leash. If this happens, accept the tiniest change to a calmer attitude and from then on use the following alternate method. Equally effective to foot tethering is to remove yourself from the puppy by stepping over one of the baby gates you undoubtedly have in every doorway. Do not talk to the wild puppy as you step over the gate or step into an X-pen. Don't even look at the puppy but just wait until the puppy acts curious as to why you left. When he calms, return over the gate and praise him. If that starts the lunacy again, yup, you go back over the gate where the puppy can't reach you.

The chew deterrent mentioned above is to stop the relentless destruction of seemingly uninteresting household articles that, for some inexplicable reason, beg the puppy to bite, puncture, shred and destroy. The spray must be well shaken, often, in a sort of a spray, shake, spray, shake application routine which must be repeated at least every twenty-four hours. I spray the edges of woodwork, the corners of rugs, the pile of magazines in the corner or whatever the puppy decides should be destroyed. I even will spray my own shoes if I am so inclined. Most pups hate the smell and taste of this bitter condiment. They sort of shake their heads and sneeze and find something else with which to entertain themselves. Let me caution you not to put bitter apple on your hands even if your puppy is biting at them. Once you get this awful tasting liquid on your fingers, you will taint the cookies you will give your puppy, which is not a good thing. Don't use bite deterrents on the leash because holding the leash with your hand will allow the bitter taste to transfer to your fingers. Never spray the bite deterrent at the puppy since it is dangerous for his eyes. Make sure plenty of safe puppy toys, such as kongs, antlers, and durable nylabones are available as appropriate chew items.

Look at What Your Breed's Job Is

Now that you can safely put the pup in a crate, at least briefly, or stand effectively on his leash, or remove yourself from those relentless teeth by stepping over a baby gate or hiding briefly in the bathroom, you have a chance to think. Hopefully you thought about the breed that was right for you BEFORE you purchased or rescued your puppy, but now it is time to give this issue more consideration. Certain breeds are hard-wired with corresponding behaviors. Retrievers, such as Labs and Golden Retrievers, are called retrievers because they, how shall I say it, retrieve. Herding dogs, such as Border Collies and Shelties, belong to that group

Mike with Boo, his Papillon lap dog and his trusty service dog Paxton.

Paxton retrieving Mike's keys.

of dogs because they herd sheep and cows or, if nothing else is available, young children. I will never forget watching a youth soccer game one day that was being played on the grounds of a working farm. The Border Collie on the premises was participating, in a Border Collie sort of way. Non-doggy spectators thought, logically, that he was going after the ball. Those of us familiar with herding dogs knew he was frantically trying to keep the ball and both teams of scattered kids all together, as any good herd should be! This scenario was frustrating for all involved, to say the

20

Fran and her retriever Dove playing with a throw toy.

least.

Terriers are bred to be ratters, wired to hunt down rodents, remove them from their hiding places and eliminate them. They are not a good choice if you have a pet gerbil or a white rat since you will end up having a Terrier - just a Terrier!

Believe it or not, some breeds are lap dogs and are bred to adorn you whenever you are in a seated position. Papillons are an example, as they were bred to be companions to royalty. If you have a Queen or two around, make sure you also have a Pap to keep her company.

The point here is that you should be aware of the breed specific behaviors you may witness in your puppy. Don't be surprised when slimy tennis balls mar your lap if you chose a Lab or when your Sheltie nips at the heels of neighborhood kids playing in your backyard. You can certainly train around these innate tendencies, but completely eradicating them may be difficult, at best. Here again management plays an important role. You may want to take your herding dog for a walk while your kids play soccer. If you own a retrieving breed, you may want to put all the tennis balls away before you put on a silk skirt to go out to dinner. You may want to have your Terrier in a crate when your rodent pet is running around the house. These are all examples of managing breed tendencies before full training has been accomplished.

I don't mean to imply that Terriers can't be taught 'Leave It' and that

Dan and Mavic, both of whom just wanna have fun.
Photo by Susan Young

Pam's Abbie resting after a long field run, a must for Border Collies and B.C. mixes. Photo by Pamela Natale

Lucia's Bella hunting for a barn rat as Wire Fox Terriers do.
Photo by Terry Chenaille

herding dogs can't be a member of a family with kids. It is just wise to be aware of what you are seeing in your puppy, why you are seeing it and then dealing with it through effective training and management. Behaviors vary breed to breed but also dog to dog within each breed. All dogs are individuals, but there are certainly traits that run in family lines and in similar breeds.

Establish House Rules (Safety First)

Keeping your puppy, your home and family safe is of utmost importance, and what I suggest you teach your puppy exemplifies this. I stress teaching pups very early in their lives to know that any object on the floor is not theirs just because it is on the floor (see Chapter 6). Dogs should know that an open door is just an open door, not an invitation to explore the world by scooting between the legs of the human and following the mailman on his route (see Chapter 8). Pups must be taught to come on a single cue, no matter what they are doing. Coming when called is not optional (see Chapter 9). Dogs must know that waste baskets contain waste, not snacks. On daily walks dogs can be ahead, exploring, and sometimes they must be behind the human: your choice, not the dogs'.

Perhaps about now you are thinking this isn't sounding like so much fun and not very positive for positive-based training. Well, believe it or not, it is. Puppies really enjoy learning, when the teaching is done by paying them when they are right instead of harshly punishing them when they are wrong. We can use many games to teach puppies just as we all learned the alphabet song to memorize our A, B, C's way back when. Clicker trained dogs can't wait to try new stuff since the

Uncovered trash can cause problems.

payoff is big and the risk is low. No collar corrections are given for "the wrong answer": just try again and if you're right next time, you get the chicken nugget! You can even help your puppy get the right answer. I always aim to make my dogs successful with gentle guidance using my voice and body language. I then build on success, end with suc-

A covered trash recepticle is a safer alternative.

cess and start the next session with a pup who is eager to learn.

Please look at your lifestyle and your home to begin establishing your safety rules. Ask yourself questions such as,

"What door will I take the puppy out to go potty?"

"Will he go out a different door to go for walks?"

"What door will I use when I am going out without the puppy?"

"Are my waste baskets covered or can they be placed too high for the pup to reach?"

"Where is a good place for dirty laundry now that I have a puppy?"

"How can I manage the amount of 'stuff' on my countertops if my puppy is getting tall very quickly?"

These sorts of inquiries lead to good management and also good decisions about what behaviors need to be taught to your pup. If you can't decide where your problem areas are, your puppy will be more than happy to make it perfectly obvious where home management needs improvement. We are about to embark on the enjoyable

Dirty laundry left on the floor is too tempting for Mensa.

Dirty laundry out of Mensa's reach.

Glitter and Mensa deciding if this lunch has been abandoned.

23

journey of keeping your home, your puppy, your children and you, safe and sound.

Create a Social Butterfly

While your puppy is young, under five months of age, it is a good idea to expose him to other puppies of different breeds. It may be possible to do this with play dates if you have friends with puppies of similar ages. However, if you want a professional present, you may want to join a puppy kindergarten at a local dog training center. Most puppy kindergartens are a blend of training your puppy in the presence of other puppies and a free play period during which the puppies get to run around in a safe and supervised environment.

If you attend a class of this sort, don't be surprised if your puppy has difficulty performing behaviors that he does readily at home. The distraction level in a class is huge, so accommodate this change by giving your puppy a lot of help, asking for lower level behaviors and using very high level cookies as rewards. In other words, if 'Sit' is a solid behavior at home to the point that you have faded out the clicker and cookies, your first day of puppy kindergarten may warrant you luring the first sit, clicking and rewarding lavishly. Fade out the lure quickly, but continue to pay success. Lowering your criteria and rewarding frequently with high value cookies will teach your puppy to pay attention to you even when a lot is going on around him. Classes are a great venue in which to accomplish this.

Chapter 2

It's Not a Remote Control
(Clicker Basics)

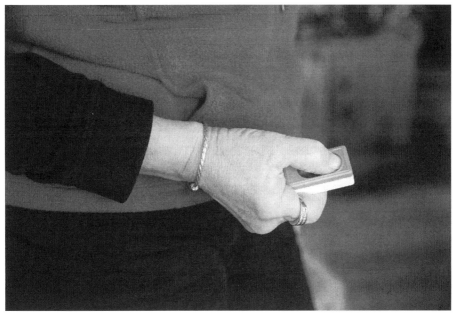

A clicker properly positioned with the thumb on the "trigger".

Now that you have decided to use an approach with your puppy that teaches correct behavior without the use of painful or fearful techniques, we need to find a good way to let your puppy know what you like. There are a lot of ways to get this done, including using your voice, using cookies and using affection. My favorite method, although it makes use of all of that, includes the use of a clicker to let your puppy know when you are happy with what he has done. Exploring how the clicker works and what its use entails will help you decide if you are going to make use of this handy tool.

Mensa being clicked for eye contact.

What exactly is the clicker? A clicker is nothing more than a little plastic box that makes a clicking sound when it is pressed. This sound is used to tell the puppy he is correct and he will be paid with a cookie for what he was doing when he heard the click. The click, in and of itself, is not a reward but the cookie is. In other words, the click is a promise for a cookie. Some people tell me that they want to use the clicking sound to get their puppy to look at them or to come back in the house from the yard. Unfortunately, it's not that easy! The clicker must never be used to GET your dog's attention. If you do this, you are "marking" what he was doing when he WASN'T paying attention. That is the LAST behavior we ever want to click. Instead, you click when your puppy is looking at you to let him know you like that. Dogs learn to work for your click. If you go to a puppy class, you can use your clicker there even if others are using a clicker with their puppies. YOUR click is the only one that matters to your puppy.

Why Use a Clicker?

There are many reasons to use a clicker. First and foremost, a click is a click is a click. A clicker isn't a male's voice or a female's voice. A clicker isn't an adult's voice or a child's voice. Everyone sounds the same when they click. Therefore, whoever clicks is a teacher to your puppy. A clicker is an equalizer in the family, making 'Mom' equal to 'Dad' and making the kids equal to the adults. This homogenizing quality of the clicker is probably reason enough to use one, but, ahhhh, there is more.

Clickers aren't charged with emotion. They don't have bad days, they don't fight with their wives, they don't get yelled at by their bosses. They don't come home and kick the proverbial dog. If you are in a bad mood and you say "Oh, good dog. Here's a cookie," but you use a sad or angry voice, your puppy will be confused that your words don't match the way you sound. If you click your dog when you are in a bad mood, the click sounds the way it always does so there is no sad voice. A click is a click is a click. No mixed message. Don't get nervous: I am not saying that you can't praise and gush and be interactive with your young canine student; you can be all of that. What I AM saying is that when you tell the puppy he is correct, it should be data and nothing more. A clicker is a perfect way to accomplish this data delivery. You can add all the emotion you want after you click and while you are giving a cookie.

The next reason to use a clicker is it's fast, just like a puppy. If your puppy sits as you hold a cookie over his head to lure him into that position, you can click the instant his little bottom hits the deck. If, instead of clicking, you say "good sit" and give him a cookie, he has probably done at least forty thousand things between the time his little butt hit the ground and the chicken hit his palette. Picture a young gymnast wavering on the balance beam, wondering when she is perfectly erect on the equipment. What better way to catch that nanosecond of perfection than with a clicker? Now picture a puppy racing around, changing position and location so fast that you start to think you have more than one puppy! What better way to catch the nanoseconds of perfection than with a clicker. Point being, a clicker is the fastest way to catch and mark a behavior, telling the puppy when he's right. We will teach your puppy it was what he was doing when he heard the magic click which bought him the cookie. No guess work involved.

Next let's look at proximity to your student. You have to be right next to a puppy to deliver a cookie or a stroke of affection. A click, however, can be delivered from a distance. For example, you may want to teach your pup to go to a mat, or into a crate or to wait at the top or bottom of a set of stairs. You can click the desired behavior from several yards away and chuck a cookie to the pup. Alternatively, you can "bait" an area (such as a crate) with food and send your dog there. You click and your pup gets his own cookie during this "self-serve" sort of training.

Now for the scientific basis: there is a theory that the clicker actually works in the amygdala of the brain rather than the cortex. So what? Rapid, permanent learning takes place in the amygdala, which is also where the fear center resides. If you have ever witnessed the permanent damage that occurs after a single, really scary event, you have seen what I am talking about. If a baby gate accidentally falls on your puppy, he will be very afraid of baby gates for a long time. That is because this event went through the amygdala. Punishment based dog training which uses methods involving pain and fear are using the amygdala to their advantage. Harsh training works. Just because something works doesn't mean it should be done. Harsh training is unnecessary and, for me, borders on being cruel. Many scientists involved with training now believe that the same rapid learning can take place in the absence of pain and fear when a non-verbal, data driven marker such as a clicker is used. We can gain all the benefits of punishment training without the pain or fear: win/win.

Clicker Rules

As with any piece of effective equipment, a clicker comes with rules. I have run into many pet owners who have been handed a clicker and told to click and give a cookie when the puppy does something good. To work well, it's a bit more complicated, but not much. So here we go: clicker rules.

Rule number one: a clicker is not a remote control. TV fans like to hold the clicker at arm's length and point it at the dog as if changing his channel. Please don't point at the pup as you click. Why not? Well, it's rude, but that isn't actually the real reason. Dogs learn with their eyes since they are visual learners. They watch every move we make but are not as good at listening. People are amazed when their dog knows the day of the week or time of day. It is really not so amazing: they simply watch every move we make. We have zillions of visual indicators for our routines, and dogs know each and every one. Briefcase? It's a work day. Gym bag? It's Saturday. Leash? It's walk time. I actually had one dog who would run up the stairs and get on my bed when I opened a bottle of seltzer water. He had learned I poured a glass of this fizzy stuff just before I went to bed and when I got upstairs he would get his good-night cookies. Another dog would run downstairs when I threw my mascara into my makeup drawer. She knew that was the last phase of making myself look presentable and it was time to go to the woods for a run. So, the point is this: if you flail the clicker around when you are clicking, the flailing becomes the marker, not the sound of the click. They watch better than they listen.

Rule number two: you don't want to hide the clicker behind your back. Why? Hiding something on a dog makes them want to find it: the

28

old curiosity killing the cat thing. Actually, this isn't really curiosity per say. What is going on here is you kick into the instinct called seeking. The seeking instinct is primal; it's how all creatures survive in the wild. Seeking food, seeking shelter, seeking water, seeking a mate are very handy instincts of survival. If you bring a bag of groceries into the house and set it on the floor, noses will be in it before you can blink an eye. Hide a clicker behind your back, and the puppy will be concentrating on what you are hiding, not what you are teaching. Simply hold the clicker in your hand with your arm casually at your side. We want the dog listening for the click, not looking for the clicker.

Clicker held at the side, not hidden or in the dog's face.

Rule number three: every time you click you MUST give a cookie. Think of click and cookie as one event. A click is a promise for a food reward. Never break a promise to your puppy. You can only do that once and your puppy won't believe you the next time. So, if you click, you give a cookie. What if you click by accident? You got it: you give a cookie. If you click, you give a cookie, every time, no matter what.

Rule number four: click one time and only one time when the puppy does what you want. This is much more difficult than it sounds. If you've been trying to get your puppy to lie down for two weeks, and he finally does it, you want to click until your thumb falls off. The problem is this: if you begin to click more than once, it makes one click less desirable than multiple clicks. Remember, the click is just data. One click is all that is needed. If you want to jackpot your dog, you certainly can, but do it with multiple cookies delivered one at a time, not with multiple clicks. I've even taught my dogs the word "jackpot". They know when they hear a click followed by that coveted word, a party is in order. I have heard that there are trainers using clickers who are breaking this rule. These folks are clicking once for an okay performance, twice for a good performance and three times for a great job. Let's think about this.   Not only does this break the rule of every click being followed by a cookie, it also breaks the entire point of a clicker being unconditional data. The clicker works so well because it goes to the part of the brain that takes in information that requires no interpretation. Once you are causing the dog to interpret how good a job they have done by changing the number of clicks, you have UN-done the data going to the amygdala and have sent it into the cortex. If you are going to work in the cortex, you have slowed down the learning. So, it's easy: click once.

Rule number five: don't have a cookie in one hand and a clicker in the other. Imagine that I came into your home to teach you how to train your pup. When I arrived I put a piping hot cheese pizza in the middle of your kitchen table and proceeded to lecture you on dog training. How

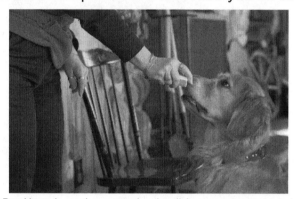

Breaking rule number one, using the clicker as a remote control.

much would you hear in the presence of melted cheese and crispy crust? Not much. A visible cookie is too distracting for the puppy to be able to pay attention to you. All he can think about is the cookie. If your cookies are in your pocket, your hand shouldn't be. How many dogs do you know who stare at your pocket if you stick your hand in it? Plenty. These dogs know where cookies are kept and were most likely trained by someone who had their hand in their cookie pocket while they were training. So, the rule is, click and then move your hand into the pocket or cookie bowl on the counter. The cookie is a reward and shouldn't be indicated until after the click is complete, unless you are luring (see Chapter 3). Enough rules? Not yet.

Rule number six: always have your thumb on the proverbial trigger when working with a clicker. If your thumb isn't resting on the clicker, ready to click, every click will be late.

Last but not least, rule number seven: don't hold the clicker down when you click but let it rebound as quickly as possible. The rebound makes another click. If you keep the clicker depressed, that rebound click will be separated from the first click and the puppy could, and probably will, move, so you will be marking a second behavior with the rebound.

Timing

I'm sure you're heard that timing is everything and clicker training is no exception. You must click as the desired behavior occurs. If you click early, you are teaching the wind-up so to speak, and, if you click late, you are teaching duration of the behavior. So, think about exactly what you want the puppy to learn and click immediately when that happens. How you get it to happen will be covered in Chapter 4, but for now just concentrate on learning how to use the clicker as a piece of equipment. Please practice your timing before you start to teach your puppy. One simple way to do this is to have someone drop an object, any object, onto the floor or a table top. You are teaching the object to land. Click AS it lands. If you click early, you are teaching it to float which is a skill the object is unlikely to learn. If you click late, you are teaching 'Stay'. If you click AS it lands, you are teaching 'Land'. It's fun to have the entire family do this exercise together. When perfection is achieved, it will sound like only one person is clicking since all the clicks are simultaneous, and all occur precisely when the object hits the table. I always know who in a family is the video game junkie, since that person will be really good at this hand/eye coordination. Finally there's a reason to play video games! Teenage boys love it when I make this announcement, much to Mom and Dad's chagrin.

Now let's get a bit more complicated. Think about teaching an animate being such a human or a puppy. They aren't as predictable as objects dropped on a table. Gravity pretty much controls the result of that scenario, but a puppy moves at lightning speed and throws in unexpect-

Practice your timing with a dropped pencil or tennis ball.

31

ed and partial behaviors. The best way to learn how to click an animate being is to use a person as the puppy. You're going to teach the person to raise his right arm as high as it will go, so that is what you click - that and only that. The person then proceeds to raise his right arm several times in a row to get you into clicking what you are teaching. The person can then start randomly raising the left arm, or only partially raising the right arm, or lifting an arm horizontally instead of vertically. None of these alternate behaviors is what you are teaching, so none of them should get clicked. Work on this until you can click immediately when the right arm is fully raised but you don't get tricked into clicking any of the other moves.

Now that you are good at clicking, you have to add giving a cookie. This is much harder and will throw off your timing again until you are well practiced. So, have a cup of M&M's or some other tiny cookie for your human "puppy". Do the arm raising exercise again, but now, every time you click your student, you deliver an M&M. Your student eats his M&M and then raises his arm again. The human "puppy" can also offer un-clickable behaviors during this exercise. You should only need about half an hour to go through this entire process, not counting the time spent laughing. Skipping it will result in a lot of clicking errors and a very frustrated puppy.

As you are teaching your human with your clicker and cookies, please consider how a dog's brain and learning style differs from that of a human's. In general, most humans are generalists. A raised arm is a raised arm, which is why we tend to click when either arm is raised until we get good at only clicking the correct arm raise. Dogs are not generalists. If I may anthropomorphize for a moment, a dog's learning style reminds me of a human who is narcissistic, is a lawyer and also has ADHD. So, there you have it. Your puppy is a narcissistic lawyer with ADHD. No wonder you're having trouble house training that tornado with fur. Here's what I mean by that. Think of the stereotypic person with narcissism. That's similar to how dogs think. They are totally self-involved and self-concerned, which is why they get accused of being stubborn. Dogs are not stubborn. They couldn't be stubborn if they wanted to be. They are persistent. Dogs know what they want and they are very persistent about getting it, but they are not stubborn. They are narcissistic. All you have to do is give them what they want, AFTER they do what you want. Simple.

Now for the lawyer part: a pup, like a talented lawyer, is a stickler for details. He gets off on technicalities. Puppies learn exactly what we teach them; nothing more, nothing less. That can be embarrassing when you realize some of the misbehavior in your puppy has been trained to occur, by you, by accident. Many people reinforce all the wrong behaviors, not because they mean to but because they don't realize what puppies find reinforcing. The human voice, eye contact, laughter and human touch all reinforce behavior. Even yelling at a puppy is reinforcing in a class-clown attention sort of way. But I digress, so back to the lawyer analogy. Puppies think in great detail. Each paw is not equal but an entity in and of itself. For example, if you want a puppy to offer its paw and always click when it raises its right paw, that is the paw it will continue to offer. If you randomly click either paw, he will randomly offer either paw. See what I mean? So, click exactly what you want to teach: exactly. As for the ADHD piece, if you saw the movie UP, you know what I'm talking about. Lade-da, ladeda SQUIRREL!!!!!! There you have it: puppies get distracted very easily and then they become ridiculously obsessed with what distracted them. It isn't that they don't come when you call them; it's that they don't even hear you when they are distracted. Until, that is, you teach them to function in the face of distraction. All in good time.

Rewards

Once you click, you must reward. "What do I use as a reward?" you ask. Well that depends on your dog. Toy obsessed retrievers might want a tennis ball throw as a reward, while a less active pup might want a hunk of chicken. A scratch under the chin might do it for some, while liver is the cookie of choice for another. All that is required for a reward to be rewarding is that the dog must love it and be willing to work for it. The word "reward" is synonymous with food, affection, attention or play, depending on what your dog enjoys. Within each of those groups, there are levels of desirability. Some dogs like cheerios better than roast beef, some like cheese balls better than liver. Tennis balls might be "better" than tug toys, and a gentle stroke might be better than a rough and tum-ble approach to petting. Only your dog can tell you what he likes and you must listen.

Don't get caught in a reward rut or even the best reward can become routine. If using different types of food, they don't need to be packed separately. With dogs, this isn't a concern. When a human smells beef stew, they may say "Oh, that stew smells good". When a dog smells beef stew, they say "Oh, those carrots and potatoes and chunks of beef smell good." Detailed thinkers, right down to the stew! However, if you want to use different 'levels' of food rewards, you may want separate con-tainers so that you know what you are grabbing. Little baggies or small plastic containers with lids work well for food separation. Toys should also be varied, and the best offered for the hardest level of work. The age old adage that 'a change is as good as a rest' applies here. I have had dogs that needed the food reward to be switched every ten minutes for them to continue to learn with enthusiasm. Every dog is different and has different preferences. You want to become very tuned into your pup to notice and accommodate his desires and he will pay you back with enthusiastic training sessions. I keep food in my cheek, tennis balls down my blouse, tug toys tucked in the back of my pants and bowls of cookies on top of every piece of furniture in the room. Life is good when cookies come in many forms and from unpredictable places. Remember, however, the cookie you deliver after a click MUST be desirable to the pup. Many of the rewards discussed above are actually conditioned, meaning the dog was taught to like them. Once the dog likes the item, it can be used as a reward. For example, some puppies love to play tug. If so, tug can be used as a reward. Some puppies don't like to tug in the beginning, but can be taught to enjoy tug. Tug cannot be used with such a puppy until he does, in fact, find tug rewarding.

Fading the Clicker

Clicking and giving a cookie is not faded out by clicking and NOT giving a cookie. Think of click and giving a cookie as a unit. It comes together and it goes together. When fading out the clicking and giving a cookie, it is imperative that it be done slowly and randomly. If a newly learned behavior is suddenly left unpaid multiple times in a row, the behavior will fade along with the paycheck. Slot machine style reinforcement (random and variable) will serve you well as your student moves along his learning curve. What I recommend is 100% rate of reinforcement while a new behavior is being taught. I continue this 'click and giving a cookie every time' routine until the behavior is quite solid on a verbal cue or a hand signal. Once the behavior is reliable, I begin my variable reinforcement which means sometimes I click and give a cookie and sometimes I do not click OR give a cookie but, instead, only praise the puppy. As I continue fading my use of the clicker, I click and give a cookie less and less often over the period of a couple of weeks. If the puppy starts to sense this fading out of rewards, I might go back to 100% rate of reinforcement for a day and then start fading again. After this fading is complete, the desired behavior is no longer clicked and given a cookie at all. As you can see, the clicker is used to teach new behaviors and can be used in this way for the rest of the dog's life. Do not, however, continue to click and give a cookie for learned behaviors. Think of the clicker as a set of training wheels which are no longer needed once riding the bike is mastered. If a behavior becomes stale, get the clicker out and click and give a cookie for that rusty behavior for a day or two as a remedial method.

All in all, using a clicker is the fastest way to teach a dog a new trick, so to speak. I find it the best way to "talk" to my dog in a way they understand and, if they understand, they learn. With a little practice, you will get good at using a clicker and your puppy will get good at doing what you want him to do.

Chapter 3

What Was That?
(Clicker Conditioning)

Some choices for food rewards: string cheese, bite size dog treats, dehydrated beef pieces and lamb lung.

A clicker is a very effective behavior marker. The first step in using a clicker is to teach the puppy what the click means. We want the puppy to know the click means he's getting a cookie, but we don't want him to think this miracle feast is an accident. We want to teach the puppy he did something to cause the click that earns the cookie. Although at first this sounds like a formidable task, it is really quite simple.

Choosing Your Cookies

When choosing what to use for food rewards, keep in mind that your pet is primarily a carnivore. Carnivores might be willing to eat Cheerios, but using such grain based stuff as a reward is not the best idea: it just isn't valuable enough. I usually use tiny pieces of boiled or baked chicken with puppies since this is easy to digest and is a meat that is the least likely to cause tummy upsets. If you don't want to use chicken, make sure what you use smells good, is soft and breakable, and easy to swallow. You might have been told that using "people food" will cause your puppy to beg at the table. It won't. What makes your puppy beg from the table has nothing to do with the food but with your behavior when you are eating at the table. Puppies do what works for them. If they bark at you when you are eating a meal and you feed them from the table, begging works and they will beg. So, long story short, using chicken is not going to cause undesirable behaviors. The cookies can be in a dish on a table in the room where you are training, or can be in your pocket in a baggie. Where the food is kept while you are teaching really makes no difference as long as it isn't in your hand until after you click.

Powering the Clicker

Powering the clicker means to teach the puppy what the click means. The best technique to teach the puppy what he is doing when he hears the click is what earns him the cookie, is a fun activity I call the 'Name Game'. Most puppies pick up how to play the game very quickly and, over a couple of days, begin to learn it is what they are doing when you click that really matters.

To begin the 'Name Game', have some irresistible cookies available. Simply say your puppy's name in an enthusiastic voice which will most likely cause him to look at you. When his eyes meet yours, click. Now go get a tiny cookie, show it to your puppy, and have him run to you to receive his treat. Praise all you want as he eats his tidbit and then release him from the exercise with a clear release such as the word "Done". Do you have to use the word "Done"? Of course you don't. Some people use "Break", some use "Release", some use "Finished", and, much to my dismay, some use "Okay". The last choice is the worst choice, in my opinion. Why? Picture this: the Fed Ex guy rings your doorbell. You ask your dog to 'Sit' and 'Stay' while you open the door. While in conversation with the delivery man, he asks you to sign for the package and you reply "Okay" and wonder why your dog runs out the door and jumps in the Fed Ex truck. He did so because you told him he was done with his 'Sit' / 'Stay'. When a dog is put on cue, all he has to do is listen for his release to know he is done. If that word is a conversational word that you may use when talking to someone other than your dog, you can accidentally release him. Pick any word you want for your release EXCEPT the word "Okay".

Back to the 'Name Game'. Let's review each step of the process described above, just as your detail thinking puppy will see it.

- You say his name.
- He looks.
- You click.
- You go get a tiny cookie.
- You offer the cookie to your puppy, backing away from him.
- He comes to you and takes it.
- You say "Done" and disengage from your pup.

Each and every step of this game has a purpose. Saying his name is what you are teaching. When you say your pup's name he is to respond with "Yes, ma'am, what would you like me to do?" He does this by looking at you. When he looks at you, you click since he has done the behavior you want. You go get the cookie since it is not visible until after you have clicked. Now you offer the cookie to the puppy to lure him to come to you to receive it. This coming forward by the puppy is very important in establishing the relationship of teacher/student. It is a "Come up to my desk for your graded paper" message. It is also the beginning of always having your puppy come to you for good things to happen. Giving the puppy the cookie from your hand is the act of rewarding for the click, as is the praise. Saying "Done" is the end of the behavior, exhibited by you disengaging from the puppy. This is another school analogy for establishing yourself as your puppy's teacher. The message is "Don't leave my classroom until the bell rings". Ending every behavior is as important as the behavior itself. If you don't tell the puppy when he is done, you give him the responsibility to decide when the behavior should end. A good example is telling your puppy to 'Sit' but not telling him when 'Sit' is over. How long does 'Sit' last???? If you don't teach a release word, you are teaching 'Sit' lasts until your puppy doesn't get yelled at when he gets up. In other words, 'Sit' lasts until the phone rings, the doorbell chimes, the oven timer goes off or another event occurs to take your attention off your puppy. He will learn he can end the behavior as soon as you are too busy to notice. Please teach a release and don't forget to use it. I recall one Fourth of July party in my back yard when we all gathered to have our picture taken, dogs included. I put them on 'Sit' / 'Stay', we took the picture and all dispersed. A bit later, a guest asked me why my dogs were sitting at attention in the middle of the yard, all by themselves. Yup, you guessed it: I never said "Done". Boy, did I feel dumb.

As you play this little 'Name Game', you will notice that your puppy starts following you around staring at you. Although sometimes saying his name and clicking when he is already looking is fine, you don't want to do this capturing style of training too often. If you can't get your puppy's eyes off of you, try kicking a toy that's on the floor or dropping something to get your puppy to look away from you. As soon as he averts his gaze, say his name and click when he looks. Now, what if you do something so distracting that he fails to look when you say his name? Well, you don't click, you don't give a cookie, and, most importantly, you don't say his name again. When talking to dogs, and teenagers for that matter, repeating yourself is a fatal mistake. Saying a cue over and over to your puppy teaches him that he doesn't have to do it when you say it since you will keep saying it until he does it. "Clean your room, clean your room, clean your room, CLEAN YOUR ROOM!" "Sit, sit, sit, sit, SIT!!!!" Both are recipes for disaster.

What DO you do if you say your puppy's name and he doesn't look? You need to be more exciting. Do or say something that will get him to look. You can use a high pitched "puppy, puppy, puppy" or clap your hands or make a kissy noise. When he looks at you in response to that attention getting gesture, click and reward. Then, instead of saying "Done" , play the game again while you still have his attention helping him to succeed and earn the "Done".

As you play the 'Name Game', it is a good idea to move around the room so that you are standing in a different spot each time you say your puppy's name. Do you know why? Dogs do not translocate what they learn. In other words, WHERE you teach them matters as much to puppies as WHAT you teach them. Say, for example, you teach your pup 'Sit' while you are standing in the kitchen, in front of the sink and repeat the 'Sit' lesson three times a day for two weeks in that same spot. You then go in the living room and ask the puppy to 'Sit.' Know what he will do? Your puppy will do exactly what you taught him to do: he will run into the kitchen and sit in front of the sink, if he sits at all. Why?: because that is what you taught him 'Sit' means. If you want a behavior to be performed in random locations, teach it in random locations from the get-go.

Schedule for Playing the 'Name Game'

Let me share some general guidelines for a teaching schedule that is usually quite successful. Teach in sessions of five to ten minutes and do a minimum of three sessions per day. You can do many more than three sessions per day, but never do more than one session per hour. Puppies actually learn between sessions. It always amazes me to see it. When I am working on a behavior that takes several sessions to teach, one of the sessions will have ended about a quarter of the way to the finished behavior, yet the puppy comes into the next session being almost half way to the goal behavior. Puppies learn when you aren't actively teaching them. They seem to mull over what you were working on, and it sort of sinks in between working sessions. It's pretty fantastic to experience it when this happens.

In addition to these five to ten minute sessions, it is really important that you do very brief training moments at unpredictable times. Making sessions painfully obvious by gathering your clicker, cookies, notes, and your puppy is an announcement that school is in session. Your puppy will learn to fold his paws on his desk during school and then eat the couch during recess! What prevents this 'school is out' misbehavior is throwing in tiny bits of training randomly throughout the day when you look otherwise occupied. Pick up the phone to talk and then turn around and say your puppy's name. Start brushing your teeth and then throw in a round of the 'Name Game'. Your puppy should never know when he is going to be asked to do something for you. It gives them something to think about other than when they can next successfully steal your underwear! When training a puppy, always have some kind of cookie and a clicker in your pocket and transfer them throughout the day from bathrobe to jeans to sweatpants and back to bathrobe. By being armed with your tools you can train for thirty seconds without having to appear to be getting ready to do so. "Keep 'em guessing", as my Mother always said.

As for fading out the clicker, there is a fairly set way to do this with the 'Name Game'. Play the 'Name Game' only inside for the first three days. During these three days use a one hundred percent rate of reinforcement (click and give a cookie every time he looks when you say his name). On day four, when playing the 'Name Game' indoors, begin variable reinforcement by sometimes clicking and giving a cookie and sometimes praise without a click or a cookie. Also on day four, begin playing the 'Name Game' outside, but with a one hundred percent rate of reinforcement. Outside is a Disney World of distraction for your puppy. Even though he seems to be doing the 'Name Game' beautifully inside, outside is much harder. Heck, out there are leaves and grass and birds and SQUIRRELS! Going back to a one hundred percent rate of reinforcement will keep your puppy in the game, literally, when faced with all of these delectable alternatives. It is also wise to choose a time of day that offers the fewest distractions. Don't go out to the kids' bus stop and expect success. Begin on your front porch, then the sidewalk in front of your house and work your way up to the bus stop over several days. Once you begin to see success, fade the clicker and cookies in the less active outdoor areas first, gradually eliminating the use of the clicker completely, anywhere outside.

Alternatives to Using a Clicker

There are situations when using a clicker may not be the best way to let your puppy know when he's right. Maybe your puppy is very noise sensitive and the click startles him. Maybe you have problems with your hands such as arthritis or trigger thumb. Maybe you don't believe you are coordinated enough to use a clicker. Don't despair….there are other ways to mark behaviors.

Let's say noise sensitivity is the issue. If you are using a box style clicker, try a button clicker. This modified device makes a slightly softer click. Another way around this problem is to keep your hand in your pocket as you click. This really muffles the sound and may be enough to put your puppy at ease. Another idea is to use something that clicks in a very soft 'tone of voice'. Try a ball point pen. You will likely be able to find a pen that clicks so softly it won't bother your pup. It is worth experimenting a bit to try to stick with a mechanical click that is not a human voice to keep all the benefits of the impartial, unbiased marker.

If noise isn't the issue but you find it physically difficult to use the clicker, you may have to go to a verbal marker. If so, using the word "Yes" in a crisp tone of voice is the best choice. You want to keep the word from taking on emotion. Saying "Yes", always the same way, keeping it brief, sharp and clear, works the best. Although I am partial to using a mechanical clicker, I will admit that sometimes anyone can get caught in a clickable moment and not have a clicker. For this reason, it is wise to develop a verbal marker of "Yes" even though you will usually be clicking. Although not as effective as a click, a "Yes" marker is always with you, so you won't miss any of those teachable moments. There will also be a few behaviors you will be teaching your puppy that won't require the use of the clicker. The two main reasons for this are 1) we don't want to use a cookie or 2) we can't properly mark the behavior with a click. House training is an example of the latter: if you click while a puppy is piddling outside, he will stop piddling to come for his cookie. It is not a good idea to interupt toileting, so don't use a clicker for house training.

Once you have taught your puppy what the clicker means, you are on your way. The sky is the limit. You can teach your puppy to do anything that doesn't require a thumb. Not only have you established an effective way to tell your puppy when he is correct, but you have also established your relationship of teacher/student with him. So, here we go......

Chapter 4

How Do I Teach That?
(Teaching Methods)

Rob luring a sit with 3 month old Kendall.

There are various ways to get your puppy to do what you want him to do so that you can click and reward. Some methods work better than others for certain behaviors. Some methods are quicker than others, but the results might not be the best product. Before you decide which method to use for which behaviors, it is important to understand what your choices are, how each one works, and the pro's and con's.

Luring

One of the quickest ways to get a behavior is by luring. This method is simply using a visible cookie to get the puppy to do what you want him to do by following the cookie. The behaviors that are the easiest to lure are positional behaviors such as sit, down, stand and those that involve moving such as walking on a leash or going to a mat. The biggest benefit of luring is the quickness of obtaining a clickable behavior. Your puppy simply follows the cookie giving you the position or location you want and, there you have it, your reason to click and give a cookie. Luring allows for a rapid rate of reinforcement which is simply a lot of cookies for little effort. This hints at the possible con of this method, namely a lot of cookies for little effort! If you lure for too long, the puppy can get addicted to this constant barrage of food and actually learn very little. When you use luring, you need to move on quite quickly to avoid having a puppy who will only sit when you hold a cookie over his head. This puppy has not learned how to sit, but simply how to eat in a seated position!

When you are using a lure to promote learning, begin by paying close attention to how you hold the cookie since the position of your hand and the movement you make is becoming a signal for the behavior you want. Once you have lured a behavior a few times, try holding and moving your hand just as you did when you had a cookie, but have no cookie. If you keep holding a cookie, it will actually become part of the hand signal to sit. If the puppy does what you want, click and then produce your cookie. This is a way to tell your puppy that the reward doesn't have to be visible before the behavior happens. You are telling your puppy, "See,

Luring Kendall into a 'Down' position.

I did have a cookie for you. You just couldn't see it." You are a sort of human pez dispenser providing a reward when the puppy does what you want. As learning happens, you go from rewarding every time to rewarding sometimes, to the finished product of a learned behavior happening when you ask for it, pay check not required. You can always go back to clicking and giving a cookie if the behavior gets stale.

Shaping

There are some behaviors that cannot be lured simply because following a cookie will not produce the behavior. An alternative here is to shape the behavior using a clicker and cookies. Shaping can be a bit tedious so you will have to be patient and trust that it does work. Shaping is done by taking the finished behavior you want to teach and breaking it down into tiny steps. Each step is taught in succession until you have the entire behavior in place. Let's take an example. Say you want to teach your puppy to push a kitchen drawer closed with his nose. Here is how you would go about shaping that behavior. Choose an empty drawer that is nose level with the puppy. Slide the drawer open and stare at it. If the puppy turns his head toward the drawer, even if it is just a head turn to see what you did, click and give a cookie. Stare at the drawer again. Wait for the puppy to look at the drawer and click and give a cookie. After three to five clicks, most puppies will figure out that looking at the drawer gets a click and they will begin to offer looking at the drawer. Once this happens, we up the ante, so to speak. The next time the puppy looks at the drawer, just continue to stare at the drawer and don't click. The puppy will then exaggerate his behavior to get you to notice he is staring at the drawer. The puppy, thinking you have gone into some kind of semi-coma, will either bark at the drawer or at you, or move closer to the drawer, or paw at the drawer or bump the drawer with his nose. If he barks, don't click since that is not a small step toward closing the drawer with his nose. If he touches the drawer with his paw, and you want him to use his nose, don't click. If, however, he chooses to touch the drawer with his nose or, by some miracle, pushes the drawer with his nose, click and give a cookie. You have now moved closer toward the finished product. Once the puppy is touching the drawer with his nose, you never again click for just looking at the drawer or you'll lose the progress you've made. Once the nose touch is reliable, stop clicking that and wait for a nose push and so on and so on until the puppy is closing the drawer. Soon you can begin associating a word or verbal cue with the finished behavior so that you can ask the puppy to close the drawer. Once the behavior is reliably on a verbal cue begin to fade the click and cookies. Voila, you have a puppy who helps out in the kitchen.

Shaping reminds me of the game we used to play as kids called the hot and cold game. Someone would think of an object in the room and the other child would have to touch that object. We used the word 'cold' to mean you were way off target and the word 'warm' to mean you were going in the right direction and the word 'hot' to mean you were very close to the correct object. With the puppy the click is the 'warm' and the lack of a click is the 'cold'. When the pup does the finished behavior, I suggest giving a jackpot where one click is followed by giving many cookies one at a time. The 'one at a time' is important. A handful of cookies is 'one' to a puppy, namely one handful. Five cookies, given separately, are five and a jackpot. When you can't think of how to train a puppy to do a certain behavior, you can usually shape it. Give it a try.

Capturing

Capturing a desirable behavior is yet another way to teach a puppy. Depending on the behavior, this can be more tedious than shaping, but can yield good results and can work when nothing else will. Capturing is exactly what it sounds like: it is capturing the moment the dog just happens, all on his own, to do what you want him to do. Believe it or not, that actually does happen! Say, for example, you want your puppy to stop whining. There is no way to lure this behavior and there is also no way to shape it. There are times, however, when the puppy is not whining. What you have to do is capture those quiet moments with a clicker and put a word on the clicked behavior for the puppy to learn. At the risk of being obvious, let's use the word 'Quiet'. I like to combine two different scenarios in this example. One is when the puppy just isn't whining. Look at the puppy, say the word "Quiet" and click and give a cookie. The puppy is a bit confused but is most certainly willing to take the cookie. Then look at the puppy again, say "Quiet" and click and treat again. Now the puppy thinks you have completely lost your mind, but again is quite willing to play your new game. Do this sort of training briefly and often. All you are doing is associating the word "Quiet" with the puppy not making any noise, although the puppy doesn't yet have a clue as to what the heck you are doing. The second scenario occurs when the puppy is whining. As he whines, refuse to look at him and just stand there, looking away from the puppy. If the puppy stops whining briefly, instantly click, say "Quiet" and give the puppy a cookie. This brief break in whining can be as quick as when the puppy inhales to whine some more. Click the inhale. If you have been saying that same word when the puppy has been quiet on his own, he will now recognize the word when you say it when he stops whining. "Got it!", he says to himself. Apparently being quiet and becoming quiet are the same thing. This is when learning begins. If whining starts up again, immediately look away and ignore the behavior. The puppy only gets clicked and reinforced when he is quiet, never when he is whining. You then, of course, must build duration or the puppy will learn to whine so he can stop to get you to click. You DON'T want to teach the puppy to whine and stop and whine and stop and whine and stop. You want to teach 'Quiet'. So once you have begun clicking short breaks in the whining, you then shape the duration of quiet by upping the ante and only clicking longer and longer durations. Don't only GET quiet but STAY quiet. Pretty good, huh?

Are you beginning to feel the puppy bonding occurring as you're teaching? You are working together, building a relationship based on learning, lots of cookies and positive feelings. Hard to beat!

Chapter 5

No More Accidents
("Toilet" Teaching)

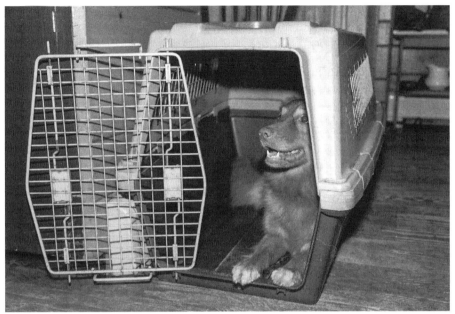

Use of a crate for house training can be very effective.

One of the first projects to take on with your new puppy is that of teaching him where he is allowed to relieve himself. Puppies poop often and pee even more often than that. They also have absolutely no idea that using your home as an outhouse is not going to work. It is your job to teach them what will work and earn them a cookie. This can be accomplished quite quickly when your approach is clear and consistent.

Indoor Bathroom is Not an Option

Puppies pee and poop whenever and wherever they want to, with one exception: where they sleep is preprogrammed as a no-pee/no-poop zone. Just as they are very detailed about everything else, they are also very detailed about this. Where they sleep means exactly that: the very small space that they fill while they sleep. If they sleep in an open area, even just two feet from where they are curled into their snoring ball of fur can serve as the master bath.

The first helpful tool to begin the process is a crate. You have probably heard of the term crate training. To keep a puppy from soiling the house during the night or when he isn't being watched, a crate is the answer. A crate should not be thought of by the puppy or the human as a jail meant for solitary confinement. When properly introduced and used, a crate is a Calgon "take me away" moment, a private sanctuary of peace and tranquility. So how do you accomplish that? Begin by using cookies to coax your puppy into a crate so it's a good place right away. Toss in a cookie, let your puppy run in and get it and invite him to join you again. No need to shut the door. Repeat this several times, finally shutting the door briefly while your pup is eating his snack. When he turns around to run out of the crate and sees the door is closed, give him a cookie through the door and then open the door and let him come out. End of session. Repeat this scenario many times throughout the day gradually increasing the time the door is closed. By nightfall, your tired little guy won't be surprised when you close the crate door for the night.

Bedding in a crate is inappropriate for a young puppy who may soil the absorbant bedding.

Where you keep the crate is an important decision. My preference, especially for overnight use, is next to your bed. Dogs are social, bonding creatures which is why we love them and desire them as companions. Bonding creatures don't sleep alone. If your puppy is crated next to your bed, he will be comforted by your scent and the sound of your breathing during the night, making it more likely he will stay asleep than if he is banished to a solitary sleep space. The only time it may not be wise to crate your pup overnight in your room is if you plan on not allowing him in that space when he is an adult dog. Once he's in, he's in, so to speak, and it will be difficult to change at a later date.

You may not like this, but no matting or bedding should be in the crate until your puppy knows he is to keep his crate dry and clean. Remember we talked about the fact that puppies don't pee in the small space where they sleep? That's true, but bedding messes with this, literally. If there is soft, absorbent material in the crate, the puppy will sleep on part of the bedding and use a small corner as a bathroom. The crate mat will prevent the urine from flowing into the spot where the puppy sleeps so he has created a master suite for himself, all in the confines of his crate. If the crate is without bedding, the urine will cover the floor, going against the natural instinct to keep the sleeping area pristine. Next time he needs to pee, the pup will whine to wake you up to take him out of the crate.

Plan to take your puppy out during the night when he whines until his body is old enough to make it through the night. Once overnight is on the road to success, we also need to tackle the daylight hours. The puppy needs to be taught that outside is where he will be going to the bathroom, whether he is in a crate or running around playing with his human companions.

Preventing Indoor Accidents

Whatever you are teaching your puppy, it is important to ensure he succeeds. Otherwise, he's doing the opposite of what you want. Practicing unwanted behavior is not advised, including where he is to pee and poop. Obviously, you don't want your puppy going to the bathroom inside, but if you want to limit the outside bathroom activity to certain areas of the yard, do this from the beginning. Consider all times of day and all times of year when you choose your outdoor area. Your puppy can't use it if he can't get to it due to snow or if it isn't safe in the dark of night. Easy access and easy cleanup are also important, so a spot where you can house a covered receptacle, lined with a small trash bag, makes sense. If you want the ultimate in convenience, a doggy door into a securely fenced area that also has a door for human access is the best plan. This allows for a twenty-four hour a day bathroom whether you are home or not, once your dog is allowed to stay loose in your house when you are absent. Now let's move on to preventing accidents inside.

As we discussed earlier, puppies pee whenever and wherever they want to do so. They have no concept we think this is wrong. They are dogs and urine is a sort of tool used to claim space as their own and make a house a home. When we enter a new space we want to make ours, we hang pictures on the walls and put our belongings on the shelves. Dogs make a space their own by peeing. Yup, peeing. While an interesting concept, we want to convince them it is unnecessary to pee indoors when living with human types. To accomplish this, diligence is needed. Unwanted bathroom activity needs to be managed prior to the puppy being house trained. Your pup should be in a crate or supervised at all times. Being in a crate is clear: the puppy is either crated or not. Supervision is a bit more complicated to explain and to accomplish. In order to supervise your puppy properly, you have to be able to see him. Pretty simple? Not really. Being able to see him involves two things. First, you must be looking at him and second, he must be confined to where you can do so. The enemy of the first issue is multi-tasking. You aren't looking at your puppy if you are watching a movie, texting a friend, making a salad or playing a computer game. The enemy of the second is the issue of physical space. Open floor plans are the worst case scenario. If you don't have a door to close, you can't easily keep the puppy in the same room with you. Don't panic. We can do it together. Let's look at the two problem areas separately.

First we'll consider how to watch or look at your puppy. The best way to ensure you are looking at your puppy is to be playing with him. Hold toys for him to chew or squeak, cuddle him, stroke him, brush him, play with his feet and tail and ears. Getting him used to interacting with you and being touched all over is important for many reasons, but it also means you are supervising him. Bonus deal. What about situations such as making or taking a phone call or getting some of those many emails read and answered? Unless you have eyes in the back of your head, these sorts of tasks require you to stop looking at your puppy and you are no longer supervising. This allows the possibility of a bathroom accident. So be it. If you want zero accidents, the puppy must be crated. If you can put up with a few minor indiscretions (which you will know how to deal with soon), that's okay too. Personal choice. Go for whatever you prefer, and

54

it can vary day to day and hour to hour. You can go for more crate time which restricts your puppy but you have fewer accidents or less crate time which is more freedom for your puppy but you will have more accidents.

When your puppy is inside and being supervised, you are available to take him out whenever you think he needs to relieve himself. Some predictable situations are:

- every hour to hour and a half when he is awake
- ten to twenty minutes after a meal
- he is sniffing around the floor or the perimeters of the room
- he tries to leave the room you are in together
- he starts racing around wildly: "the zoomies"

Paying attention and getting your puppy outside prior to an accident is a big part of successful house training. Remember we talked about not letting your puppy practice behaviors you don't like? Peeing in the house is a good example. Every time he goes to the bathroom inside, he is practicing something you don't like. Every time you get him outside to go, he is practicing something you do like. Let's make it worth his while to go outside by paying him to do so. Each and every time your puppy pees or poops in the yard or on a walk, give him a cookie and identify what he did with a "pee" or "poop" word. Teaching him words that relate to his elimi-nation will later allow you to ask him to pee or poop. Once he knows the words and you ask him to relieve himself using the words, he will do so if he needs to. This saves a lot of time outside in the rain or the dark and also allows you to have him empty before he is left home alone without bathroom access. Obviously, you have to have a cookie with you when you take your puppy out in order to pay him for using his outdoor bath-room. If, for some reason, you can't have cookies in your pocket all the time, keep a jar of cookies at the door so you can take a few on your way out.

When you take your puppy out because you think he needs to go, don't stay outside too long waiting for the blessed event. When you get outside, if your puppy pees right away, give him a cookie, tell him he peed and let him play outside a bit if he enjoys doing so. If he then does a bowel movement, give him another cookie, tell him what he did and, again, let him play a bit in the yard. If, however, when you take him out he just wants to play and not go to the bathroom, don't stay out more than one minute for a pee break or more than five minutes for a poop break. Bring him back in and crate him or watch him like a hawk. Five minutes later, bring him out again but only for a few minutes. If he still doesn't go, bring him back in the house. Keep doing this until he either starts to piddle on the floor so you can grab and run outside or until he pees on one of his brief outdoor opportunities. Then give him a cookie and let him play outside. Remember how a puppy thinks: very detailed and self-involved. If, every time he pees or poops, you immediately bring him inside, he will figure out the routine: he goes to the bathroom and goes back in the house. If he refuses to relieve himself when you take him outside and you stay outside waiting forever for him to go, he figures that out as well: if he doesn't go, he will get to stay out. See where I'm headed? Puppies learn to "hold it" to get you to stay outside with them so they can eat sticks and play with the mulch and chase birds. People have told me their puppies have trained them to stay outside for forty-five minutes before piddling. Avoid getting into this routine. It's better to reward a puppy with outside playtime for relieving himself quickly than for holding it! This being said, there are puppies that hate to be outside. These pups will not try to stay out longer but will pee or poop quickly in order to go back in the house. Their reward is to go back inside.

As you can see, preventing accidents is a proactive process. It involves crating your puppy, supervising your puppy and getting your puppy outside when needed. The more accidents you prevent, the better, but you won't be able to prevent them all. So, then what?

Interrupting Accidents

No matter how well you think you are watching your liquid filled pet, you will inevitably catch him starting to squat. When this happens, grab and run. Scoop your puppy up, right in middle of him squatting on the kitchen floor, and run for the door. Make sure you have cookies so you can pay him for a successful trip. Even if he started to pee inside but finishes outside, he gets paid. These interrupted accidents make a big impression on your canine student, and an even clearer point than just bringing him out so often that he never has an accident. Every time you swoop up your pup and whisk him out the door as he is starting to go, it is a wonderful lesson: don't pee inside, pee outside.

While we're talking about accidents, let's also address the human part of this equation. Although accidents are obviously the fault of the human since they only happen when supervision is faulty, it is important that the human not feel "punished". Accidents are bound to happen on everyone's watch. The puppy isn't yet house trained so it should be expected. If the person watching the puppy gets blamed every time an accident occurs, that person is going to be less and less willing to play the "watch the

56

puppy" game. To keep the list of those willing to supervise from drastically dwindling, the humans should be given full immunity. They will feel badly enough for allowing the puppy to fail without being blamed by the other humans. Don't forget, he might pee on your next watch.

Finding Accidents

So we agree, accidents happen. Expect them and deal with them each and every time. Many books and articles on house training tell you when you find an accident it is too late to deal with it. Just clean it up and do a better job of watching the puppy. This approach is faulty. If you stumble across a puddle or worse and dispose of the evidence without involving your puppy in the process, your pup has an indoor bathroom and a maid: you!

There is a very effective way to let your puppy know that piddling in the house is not okay. When you find an accident, several steps are in order. First, go get a paper towel or a baggie, depending on what type of accident you have encountered. Next, go get your puppy and put his leash on him. Take your puppy to the scene of the crime and point out the mess. Now the most important part: you get to use a whiny voice and act disappointed and simultaneously surprised at what your puppy has done. The choice of words doesn't matter but the tone of voice does. Don't sound angry. Remember what detailed learners puppies are? If you act angry, the puppy learns that you don't like to find his bathroom mistakes. He will make sure you don't find his accidents by peeing behind the couch instead of in the middle of the kitchen floor. He'll get so good at it, you won't find his accidents until you move out, pull all the furniture away from the walls and pull up the rugs. Not pretty.

Instead of anger, you want to act disappointedly surprised, sort of like when a best friend does something dumb. You can sound this way by using a whiny tone and saying phrases such as "Really??? Again???" or "This isn't a bathroom." or "I just took you out five minutes ago!" Get what I mean? Then, when you get done whining, blot up the puddle with the paper towel or pick up the poop in the baggie and take the puddle, the poop and the puppy all outside to where the event should have taken place. Blot the urine into the grass or put down the feces and it's over. In the rare event that your puppy pees again, outside, give him a cookie.

Dealing with accidents as outlined above makes it very clear to the puppy what you want since you have provided a visual example. You have very clearly stated to the puppy that if he pees in the house, he and

Pointing out a bathroom accident, after the fact.

his accident will be brought outside, interrupting his busy day and he will get no cookie. If, however, he goes to the bathroom outside, he will get a cookie. It is a no-brainer for the puppy which is the best deal. You have convinced him that outdoor bathroom duty is the way to go.

Asking To Go Out

Try not to be frustrated your puppy doesn't tell you when he needs to go out. This is actually the very last piece to the puzzle. A puppy that pees on the floor doesn't need to ask to go out since he goes to the bathroom inside. It is only after the puppy realizes going inside isn't acceptable that he will come up with a way to ask you to open the door. He may bark, whine or scratch at the door, tug on your sleeve or stare at you. I prefer to let the puppy come up with his own way to ask me to open the door. If his way is faulty, I can always teach him to ask in another way such as ringing a bell or a small wind chime placed next to the door. His way is faulty if it doesn't get my attention. If a puppy sits quietly at the back door and I am not looking his way, I don't know he needs my help. He needs a better way. If a bell or wind chime will help, I hang one of these on the door where the puppy can reach it with his nose. I put a dab of peanut butter on the bell and when the puppy makes the bell ring by licking off the sticky, tasty spot, I open the door. After several repetitions of ringing and opening, the puppy will start to understand that ringing the bell opens the door. The peanut butter smearing can be abandoned once this is understood. If your puppy abuses this privilege by ringing the bell constantly so he can go out and play, just remove the bell when you know the puppy is empty and replace the bell when you think the proper time is approaching.

Now your housetraining plan is complete. You know how to prevent accidents, what to do if you catch your puppy in the act and how to handle it if you find the results of an accident after the fact. This process will take several weeks to accomplish, but most puppies can be fully house trained by the time they are seventeen to twenty weeks old.

Chapter 6

I Can Do Anything
(Self-Control For Your Pup)

The ultimate in self control for Glitter and Mensa.

As I'm sure you have noticed, puppies have very little self-control. Delayed gratification is certainly not their forte. Puppies know what they want, they want it NOW and they can usually figure out how to get it. I have gone into homes where puppies have taught the owners to deliver cookies on demand by banging on the cookie cupboard. Unfortunately, this sort of arrangement escalates into the owners running back and forth to the cookie jar and to a very fat puppy! But, the good news is, even if this scenario has been created, we can fix it.

It is really important to establish who in the home the teacher is, and it is not the pup. The way to go about this is simple, but may not be easy at first. All that needs to be done is to show the puppy the way to get what he wants is to first do what the human wants. This simplified version of the Premack principle works miracles. Everyone is happy, human and puppy alike. Win/win.

Rules for Meals

The food bowl rules the roost so we need rules for the food bowl. A puppy can't wait to eat his meals, so let's use those meals to teach polite behavior. First of all, be sure there are actual meals with a beginning and an end, not a buffet. A puppy should eat on a schedule, not graze, for several reasons.

- One reason is house training. I can just about set my watch based on what time my dogs poop. If they ate all day long, there would be no schedule for elimination and house training becomes haphazard.
- Another reason is relationship. You are the teacher. You deserve respect. What do our scavenger puppies respect? They respect the best hunter. Establish that you provide the food and when the food is to be eaten. Bingo: you have just become the best hunter in the world. Leave the food sitting in the bowl all day, and guess who the hunter is? Your puppy. This is not the relationship you want.
- Yet another reason to feed on a schedule is the value of the food itself. When food is available all day long, it loses its intrinsic value. We use food rewards as the basis for most of our training. Food needs to be valuable, or there goes our reward base.
- One more reason for feeding on a schedule, in case you don't have enough already, is preventing the exhibition of resource or food bowl guarding. Suffice it to say that you, as the provider of food, can keep your hand on the edge of the food bowl as your puppy is eating, add to the food bowl as he is eating, pick up some of the food and hand feed it to your puppy as he is eating, and show you are not a threat to his resources. You give your puppy no reason to growl to protect what he is eating. You are right there, interacting with him as he eats and the food is never taken away from him.

Another rule for meals is for your puppy to be calm as the food is provided. This is best accomplished by being completely silent but by "talking" with the bowl itself. Hold your puppy's prepared meal in the bowl at your waist level. If he is calm, begin to lower the bowl toward the floor. If he jumps for the bowl, simply elevate it back to waist level and do not begin to lower it again until he is calm. Slowly lower the bowl for the calm puppy and elevate it for a revved puppy until you can place it on the floor. Once it is on the floor, invite him to "eat". Do not rush this process. The first time you feed this way it might take three or four minutes to get the bowl to the floor. The next time it will take one minute, and the next time he will remain calm as you place his bowl for him to eat. If you talk at all, the entire process takes longer.   If you are silent, the puppy can concentrate on what the bowl is doing which tells him what to do. This works like magic. Wow, your first lesson in teaching your puppy self-control is complete. Now on to the fun stuff.

'Leave It' / 'Take It'

One of the best routes on which to continue our journey to self-control for your pup is to play the 'Leave It' game. 'Leave It' means "Don't even think about grabbing, or worse yet, devouring, that sock/cell phone/vitamin pill/rabbit poop/acorn/burger that fell off the grill/(you fill in the blank)".   This game, once learned, not only saves many a sandwich sitting on the counter but will save a lot of vet bills as well.

Case in point: one evening I left my two older dogs home with my then teenage son and took my young dog to a training class. When I got back, I unleashed my young beast and, as I was taking off my coat, looked up to see him poised over a plate of left over Kentucky fried chicken, bones and all, that my son had left behind. My older dogs knew not to touch it, but my younger pup did not yet fully grasp all the house rules. I yelled "Leave It" and the dog stopped in his tracks and left the bones untouched. Whew! Those two words saved me a lot of worry. Now let's discuss how to teach this very important skill to your furry scavenger.

The game of 'Leave It' is played with you on the floor with your puppy. Take a chunk (tablespoon size) of food that he thinks he can't resist, such as chicken meat or a portion of a string cheese. Put the food on the floor, cover it completely with your hand, and say nothing.   The pup will try to figure out how to get the food. He will lick the back of your hand that is over the food, he might bite at your hand, claw at your fingers, or mug your hand with his nose. Don't budge, talk or even look at the puppy while all this is going on. Sit quietly on the floor, while keeping your hand still and completely covering the food. Eventually, the pup will stop trying what doesn't work and will usually, albeit very briefly, stare at your hand trying to figure out his next mode of attack. This nanosecond he stops trying to get the food gets a click. After you click, pick up the chunk of food, break off a tiny piece of it and hand it to the puppy with a "Take It" cue. The pup, although perplexed, will gladly oblige and eat the morsel. The remainder of the chunk then goes back on the floor, and is again covered by your hand. Back we go to licking and pawing and biting at your hand until the pup takes a break to rethink his plan, and again, the break gets clicked and he gets a piece of the food. After a few repetitions, the pup will start to figure out that looking at your hand is what is being clicked and the grabby behavior will begin to vanish. Once he is getting more frequent clicks for staring at your hand, begin to lift one side of your hand in a clamshell sort of way to expose the food. If the pup moves toward the food, the clamshell hand shuts, cutting off access to the food. If the pup continues to stare at the food as you expose it, say "Leave It" , click and give him a piece of the chunk. Keep opening your hand slightly to expose the food. Close it if the puppy goes for it and then try again. Click if he stares at it and then reward. At this point in the game, the progress moves at lightning speed. Within minutes, you can expose the food, say "Leave It" , the puppy keeps staring at the food, say "Leave It" again, the puppy still stares, click, pick up the food and give him a piece of it. This process is building duration so your puppy can leave the food alone for longer than a nanosecond. During all of this, never look directly at the puppy but,

Tom and Riley practicing 'Leave It' with chicken on the floor.

instead, keep staring at the food on the floor, just as you want the puppy to do. Dogs follow the human line of vision. If you want the pup to look at the food, you must look at the food.

Before we progress to the next step, let me explain why you want the puppy to stare at what you are telling him to leave. I admit this is a bit different from the way many teach 'Leave It'. Some trainers want the dog

64

to look and move away from what they are told to leave. Why do I teach the opposite? Let's look at the comparison of an overweight person who is faced with going to dinner with a friend. A weak dieter will have to avoid their favorite restaurant or their diet will go by the wayside. However, a committed abstainer can go to any restaurant and order an appropriate meal. I want your puppy to be a committed abstainer full of self-confidence so that he can stare that chunk of meat right in the face and not touch it. This does more than teach 'Leave It': this teaches a pup to think they are the smartest canine ever to hit the face of the earth and they have the smartest teacher since you taught him how to do it! If you and the pup can accomplish this, you can do anything together. There is also another reason I want the pup to stare at the food on the floor. When a pup is playing 'Leave It', he becomes almost hypnotized as he waits for you to click and give him the food he is staring at. When this behavior becomes solid, I use his concentration on the food to do things to him that he might otherwise find objectionable, such as ear cleaning, nail trimming, and brushing. This sort of trance-like behavior can come in very handy since your pup is almost frozen in time when he is playing 'Leave It'. Breaking the trance is accomplished without too much trouble. Once you put this game to the test in reality, if the pup stares at the underwear he is told to leave, just say his name and he will look up at you, as he learned to do in the 'Name Game' (Chapter 3). Now, let's move on to the next step of 'Leave It'.

Once you can have the puppy stare at the food on the floor for several seconds while repeating the "Leave It" cue, you want to begin moving the chunk of food closer to the puppy. To begin this phase of the game, have the puppy staring at the uncovered food as you say "Leave It". Then say "Leave It" again and move the chunk about a half an inch closer to the puppy. If he goes for it, simply cover the food with your hand, saying nothing. Then say "Leave It" and uncover the food. Say "Leave It" again, and move the food another half inch closer to the pup. If he continues to stare, say "Leave It" and move it, say "Leave It" and move it until you think he needs a pay check and then click, pick up the food and give him a piece of it, saying "Take It". By this time, you have most likely been training for about five or ten minutes so end the session to let the puppy rest. Just as when we played the 'Name Game', we don't want to train more than five or ten minutes at a time. Plan to have no fewer than three sessions per day. More than three sessions a day is fine, as long as you don't do more than one session per hour.

After at least an hour of rest, you can begin again. A quick warm-up review is a good idea to remind the puppy what he learned the last time. Then begin to move the food closer and closer to the pup until you actually rest the food against his paw. When you do this, the pup may withdraw his paw as if saying, "Hey, that's my foot you're messing with." If he picks up his foot, say nothing but simply pick up the food, removing the possibility for a click. When he puts his foot back down, put the food back on the floor and begin the game again. Progress until you touch his foot with the food again. If he allows it to rest there, click and jackpot (several small pieces of food delivered one at a time) but if he picks up his foot, silently pick up the food. Oh, let me caution you about another detail to the game: you may have noticed I described saying "Leave It" and then moving the treat closer. The order here of saying "Leave It" and then moving the treat is intentional. If you move the treat without saying "Leave It" first, the pup may go to grab it thinking you are moving it to give it to him. If you say "Leave It" prior to moving it, you are more clear as to what you are doing. I compare this to a doctor who is about to give you a flu shot saying "little pinch" just prior to giving the injection. He doesn't give the injection and then say "Oh, sorry, little pinch". The words are a warning and must precede the action.

As you play this game, the speed of progression is based on the puppy's behavior. What you want is the puppy to stay almost motionless during this game. The more you play, he might begin to move around while avoiding the food. This activity should resemble playing chess with your pup and chess is not an aerobic activity. The pup should not be running around or backing up or barking or doing anything but staring at the food. You don't have to specifically teach the pup to be motionless; just don't click when he is moving. I never tell the pup to sit or lie down when playing this game, but I find as a puppy becomes more committed to playing chess with me, he chooses to sit or lie down; he

Derek and Riley playing 'Leave It'.

sort of pulls up a chair to the chess board, so to speak.   If your puppy walks away or even turns his head away from the game, don't confuse this with boredom. It is actually the opposite of boredom and is the exhibition of stress. Learning is stressful. This isn't bad or wrong, it is just stress. Walking away from the game is a sort of "going to the water cooler". It is a break. If your pup walks away, pick up the food. When he returns, put the food down, resume play briefly and end the session on success.

Once your puppy can easily sit and stare at the food resting against his paw, it is time to move on. Next session, after a warm up, rest the food against his paw but, instead of clicking, say "Leave It" and move the food up onto his foot. He may object, but you know what to do: if he picks up his foot knocking the food onto the floor, simply, silently, pick up the food until he can resume. Again, work the food toward and then up onto his foot. If he goes for it, cover it while leaving it on his foot, say "Leave It" and expose it on his foot until he can stare at it on his foot. If this takes more than one session, so be it. Always work with the same foot. Remember the section on Timing in Chapter 2 when we talked about how detailed dogs are in their thinking? The narcissistic lawyer analogy? Well, this is another example of that way of thinking. To dogs, the left paw literally doesn't know what the right paw is doing. That means we have to teach one paw at a time for the 'Leave It' game. If you switch back and forth between the left paw and the right paw, it will take twice as long to teach. Once the right paw can do 'Leave It', then you can teach the left paw to do it, or vice versa. Once your puppy can do 'Leave It' with food on either the right foot or the left foot, you guessed it: two pieces of food, one on each front foot. When you click, he gets the food off both feet. What a great deal. I play this game with my dogs their entire lives. They never get sick of it since they know they always get the food when I click. I don't fade the click out of this game since I am playing with food, so I might as well click.

Having the food on your puppy's feet is not the end behavior. 'Leave It' on the feet is the warm up for throwing food around the room and having your puppy stare at flying chicken landing on the floor all around him. Yup, that's where we're headed next. Here we go.

Taking 'Leave It' Airborne

As if staring at food on his feet isn't good enough, now it's time to add even more challenge to the game. As we have discussed, teaching a puppy the skill 'Leave It' raises his self-confidence and, also, his confidence in you as his teacher. It is a safety valve for keeping him from eating non-edibles and edibles that could harm him. Teaching him not to go after food that falls off plates, gets thrown from high chairs, drops off barbeque grills and flies off cutting boards is taking this game to the next level, and a necessary level at that. We have many foods in our cupboards that are not good for our dogs and are even potentially lethal. Grapes and raisins, in fairly small amounts (seven or eight grapes or a snack box of raisins) can cause kidney failure in dogs. Onions, in a single large dose or small amounts over time, can cause liver failure. Macadamia nuts can cause temporary and sometimes permanent rear end paralysis. Caffeine and alcohol cannot be metabolized by dogs: a drunken dog can be a dead dog. A hidden source of alcohol is raw dough that contains yeast. If a dog consumes raw dough, the yeast continues to ferment and gives off alcohol inside the dog. Many hours after the initial indulgence, the dog can begin to show signs of alcohol toxicity and needs veterinary intervention. Chocolate, actually the theobromine it contains, can cause a dog to have a heart attack. The darker the chocolate, the more deadly it is. Artificial sweeteners such as Truvia, Stevia and Xylitol can be very harmful to canines. This list is not meant to scare you; well, I guess it actually is. But the purpose of scaring you is to convince you that teaching 'Leave It' to all puppies is of utmost importance. So, let's continue.

To begin the airborne 'Leave It' game, line your countertop edge with tasty morsels, saying "Leave It" as you do so. I want you to tell the puppy what game we are playing before any food starts to drop. We don't want him to show up at the Patriots game wearing a Celtics shirt, so best he know what is going on before the game begins. As you get ready to knock the first tidbit off the edge of the counter and onto the floor, notice what your pup is doing to decide how to proceed. Some pups sit facing the counter, realizing that 'Leave It' means whatever is about to happen doesn't involve them. On the other hand, some pups figure this is the chance they've been waiting for to grab what they want and stand ready to pounce. The latter pup needs a bit of assistance, so slip a finger gently in the collar before going any further. Next, put all of your body weight onto one of your feet, having the other foot ready to hover over the food if the pup goes for it. Now, knock the first piece of food onto the floor, repeating "Leave It" a few times as it falls to its final resting place. If the pup moves for it, even if your finger is in his collar, hover your foot over the food, protecting it from your furry seagull. Tell your pup to "Leave It", and as he settles into food-staring mode, expose the food and begin to remove your finger from his collar. As he stares at the food, knock a second piece of food off the edge of the counter, ready again to hover. Then a third and a fourth piece can follow. As your pup watches this process, continue to tell him to "Leave It". When you are ready, click as he stares at the food on the floor, then pick it all up and give him several cookies from a different source such as your pocket or a dish on the counter. You never want a puppy to think he will ever get what was dropped on the floor, so never give it to him. This varies from playing the original 'Leave It' game when you sit on the floor with the puppy. That food you give him. Now you don't, since the food has fallen from a prep surface or a place where you eat.

As the puppy gains experience at this game, move around so you play off every surface in the home where food is prepared, cooked or eaten. You want the puppy to know food can drop from a lot of different surfaces but that none of it is for him to grab and swallow. Begin saying "Leave It" fewer times and give less warning that a spill is about to occur. When you can say "Leave It" only once as the food falls, the training is pretty much in place, although reminder games are always a good idea. I can't begin to tell you how many times having taught my dogs this behavior has come in very handy. I drop chopped onions on their way to the skillet, M & M's on their way to my mouth, light bulbs as I remove them from their cartons, burgers off the grill, ornaments from the tree, and the list goes on. In fact, it seems I drop coffee beans so often as I try to wrestle them into the grinder that when they hit the floor, my dogs look at each other and say "Leave It". Okay, this is a bit of an exaggeration, but it seems to be that effective. To keep the behavior fresh, sometimes when I drop something and tell my dogs to "Leave It", I will give them a cookie and sometimes I don't: variable reinforcement at work.

'Find It'

Another very useful game to teach your puppy is called 'Find It'. At first glance this appears to be too easy for your puppy to even call it "teaching". But, as you look closer, you will see a lot of learning is going on. To begin the game, take several small cookies and cup them in the palm of one hand, sliding one forward to be held between your thumb and index finger so you can show one cookie to your pup. Tease him with it, getting him interested in following the cookie with his eyes as you move it back and forth and then say "Find It" in a playful voice and toss the cookie on the floor, not too far at first. The puppy will run to get the cookie and, I can pretty much guarantee, will look back at you without being asked.

That is what gets clicked: unsolicited reorientation back to you after eating the cookie off the floor. Remember, what we click is what is being taught. Here we are teaching your pup to always look back to you, no matter how much fun he is having away from you. This is another lesson in self-control to add to the 'Leave It' game which began this chapter. Back now to 'Find It'. You say "Find It", throw a cookie, your puppy runs for it, eats it and looks back to you. You click and now you must give a cookie. The way to deliver the reward for this game is to throw the next piece of food from your hand after showing it to the pup. In other words, show a cookie, say "Find It", toss it, puppy finds and eats the cookie, puppy looks back to you, click, show a cookie, say "Find It", toss it, puppy finds and eats the cookie, puppy looks, click and continue to repeat this cycle until you want to end the game. When that time comes, after you click the puppy for looking back to you, show the last cookie and, instead of tossing it, tell the puppy to take it from your hand and say "Done". Game over. As the puppy learns what the words 'Find It' mean, you can toss the cookie further and further. When you really want the food to travel, use kibble (dry dog food) which will skid across the floor for long distances. This makes the game really fun and challenging for your puppy to find the food as it 'runs' away from him. As your puppy hunts, leave him to his own devices to find his booty. If he gives up, we want to teach him that whenever you say "Find It", there really is something to find. Do this by staring at the elusive cookie on the floor, slowly walking toward it, then point to it and, if all else fails, use the universal toe tap to bring the puppy's attention to it. You are saying with your body language, "See, I told you there was a cookie there".

The game of 'Find It' is a very useful tool to have in your repertoire. Not only does it teach the main point of reorientation back to you, but it is also a great redirection game. It is fun, active for providing some exercise, and easy for the puppy to do correctly. Switch on the 'Find It' game when you need the puppy to stop doing what he is doing and there really isn't a good way to get him to do so. Examples are grabbing things and running off with them, charging the door when the doorbell rings, biting on the leash when you attach it to his collar, biting at the hem of your pants, or any of the other billion ways your puppy drives you nuts. If you grab a handful of tasty morsels and start playing a round of 'Find It', your puppy will stop what he is doing and join the game. For the redirection to be effective, however, he has to know the game to begin with. So, play for no reason other than to teach him the game and the words "Find It" and then use it to get yourself out of those inevitable situations when your puppy is doing stuff you hate.

Racquetball for Your Dog: Combining 'Leave It' and 'Find It'

Playing racquetball with your puppy is one of the most fun games you will ever play. Let me caution you the puppy must be well versed in both 'Leave It' and 'Find It' before attempting this combination of the two. It involves throwing treats and randomly telling the puppy whether to "Find It" or to "Leave It". I discovered this amazing game by accident. One of my dogs would frequently refuse breakfast for no good reason except he wanted to wait awhile. That didn't work for my schedule, and I was not going to break the Cardinal rule of meals, which is no free-feeding. Since this pup tended to be underweight, I had to find a way to get him to eat. What better way than 'Find It'. Dogs, as we have discussed, are scavengers. Eating out of a bowl is boring compared to hunting for dinner. So, I would take my picky eater into a room away from my other dog and proceed to hide his breakfast in little piles around the room and tell him to "Find It". He would run around the room happily eating the same food he found boring when it was sitting in his bowl. One particular time, as he approached a little pile of food, I thought I saw my second dog entering the area so I instinctively said "Leave It". Well, lo and behold, my hunter who had been told to "Find It" stopped dead in his tracks when I said "Leave It" and stared at the food. A new game was born: 'Find It' / 'Leave It', or racquetball for dogs.

All you need for this game is a puppy who knows how to play 'Leave It' and 'Find It' and a handful of dog food. Throw a piece of kibble and tell him to "Find It". After he eats it, throw another and tell him to "Find It". Then throw another and tell him to "Leave It" as he runs toward it. As he leaves that one, throw another and tell him to "Leave It". Once you have several pieces of food on the floor, tell him to "Find It", "Find It", "Find It", one cue for each piece of food he previously left. The first time you try this you may want a second human present to referee. If the pup goes for a piece of food you told him to leave, the second person scoops it up so that the puppy doesn't get it. Try again, until the puppy is able to follow the rules. This game is great physical and mental exercise, both at the same time, just like racquetball.

Self-control is being taught and rewarded with all of the above. Dogs only do what we reinforce so let's reinforce what we want them to do: calmly wait for their meals, leave items we ask them to leave, take items we ask them to take and have fun and get exercise along the way. Happy owner equals happy puppy and vice-versa.

Chapter 7

Ouch!!!!!!!!!!

Mensa doing a nose 'Touch' instead of nipping.

Sometimes puppies seem to be partly, or even mostly, Piranhas. They relentlessly bite at our hands, feet, socks, hems of pants and sleeves. Their teeth are needle-like and able to damage skin and clothing easily, plus it HURTS! When puppies behave this way, no one wants to be around them or play with them, particularly children who also seem to be the most likely targets. Let's start by managing this behavior which instantly controls it. Then, adding replacement behaviors gives the finished product of a pup who knows how to properly engage his humans without resorting to attack mode.

Puppies bite. Some puppies bite more than others. The causes are multiple and include attention seeking, teething, play behavior and prey drive. The reason the biting continues is pretty simple: it gets reinforced by humans, usually by accident. If a pup grabs your pant leg and you pull back, you are inadvertently playing tug, a favorite game of dogs, and, therefore, reinforcing the grabbing of pant legs. If your puppy bites your bare or sock covered foot and you jump up on a chair screeching and flailing, you have provided a wonderful show thus reinforcing the behavior with your entertaining reaction. What are you to do when you feel like a human pin cushion? Here are my suggestions.

Some puppies will accept a toy as a replacement object when they try to bite on your skin or clothing. Puppies should have a variety of toys at their disposal including antlers, durable Nylabones, raw bones (not cooked bones which splinter), stuffed toys (made for dogs since stuffed toys for children contain flame retardant) and Kongs. The latter can be

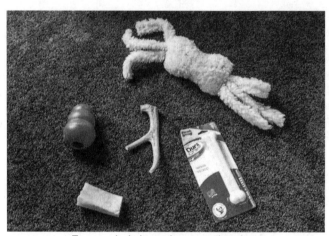

Toys can include raw bones, antlers, kongs, nylabones and tough plush toys.

stuffed with a mixture of puppy food and peanut butter and frozen for a duration treat. Offering the pup one of these toys can sometimes inhibit biting. Don't allow your pup to be alone with toys he can destroy and swallow. Only give destructible toys, such as plush varieties, under supervision, but the other choices are safe for pups to have even when crated. Unfortunately, many pups push the toy aside when in a human attack mode, so let's move on.

If you are sitting on the floor stroking your puppy and he puts his teeth on your hand, slowly and silently remove your hand from his reach, wait two seconds, and begin stroking him again. If you get more teeth on skin, remove your hand again. Since your puppy probably enjoys the stroking, once he figures out that biting you causes the stroking to stop, the biting will stop. This may take five repetitions and it may take five hundred repetitions, but it will work with most puppies.

Occasionally there are puppies who will lunge at the retreating hand and jump up and continue to bite. This may be due to removing your hand too quickly, making it look like a game. Try removing your hand more slowly. If this doesn't work, since you are sitting on the floor, stand up as you withdraw your hand. This may stop the biting long enough for you to pause and begin stroking again. If the puppy doesn't care that you stood up, turn your back. If the puppy continues to lunge and bite at the back of your legs, we need to do more: time for a shield. Yup, you need a shield. If you aren't in possession of an actual shield, which most of us aren't, I can guarantee you have something that will work.

Mensa and Glitter outside the wire X-pen for biting Jane's ankles.

Try using an extra baby gate that is not being used in a doorway, the lid of a large plastic storage bin, a serving tray, a cookie sheet, or whatever else you have on hand that is flat, lightweight, portable and is about 1 ½ by 2 feet in size. When you remove your hand from the puppy's mouth and begin to stand up, place the shield between the two of you as a barrier. Pause, remove the shield and go back to petting your puppy. Repeat until he accepts your touch without biting.

If you don't like the shield approach, or you want an additional way to protect yourself, remove yourself completely, although briefly, from the puppy. This is accomplished by stepping over a baby gate into another room, stepping into an X-pen or going into another room and closing the door between you. Reappear and disappear as needed, based on your puppy's behavior. All of this is done WITH NO TALKING. A puppy who is misbehaving does not get anything from the human: no touch, no eye

Derek using a plastic lid as a shield to prevent Riley from ankle nipping.

Derek removing the shield when Riley is calm.

contact, and no verbal interaction. Simply go away. Teach your puppy that' biting' makes you disappear but 'not biting' makes you stay. It is very simple.

What about the suggestion you may have heard to scream "OUCH!!!!!" when your puppy bites? I have found an occasional puppy this works with, but not many. Most puppies get more revved by human screeching, so I usually don't suggest it.   If you try it and it works, fine. If it doesn't work, or even makes the biting worse, don't be surprised. Another popular suggestion is to spray the puppy in the face with water. That is a technique I will not use and will not suggest for you. This is flat out punishment. It is fear-based training and I don't use fear to teach behaviors to pups or to stop behaviors. You don't want your puppy to be afraid of you or to be afraid of spray bottles which you may use for grooming purposes or to humidify your orchids. Once your puppy is afraid of any item, that item can't be used around the house without scaring him. Just because something may effectively stop a behavior, does not mean that it is the method that should be used. There is always a humane alternative.

Teaching 'Touch'

What we have talked about so far is how to manage that mouthful of needles attached to your puppy. The more we redirect the puppy and arrange the environment appropriately, the less we let our puppy practice all the biting that is so normal and natural for them but concurrently obnoxious to us. In addition to management, it is also a good idea to teach the puppy what is called replacement behaviors, so here we go.

A replacement behavior is something you teach your puppy to do that makes it impossible for him to do what you don't like at the same time. Since we are dealing with puppy nipping and an open mouth that grabs your skin and clothing, let's teach the puppy to 'Touch' your hand with his nose. This 'Touch' keeps your puppy close to you but

Glitter and a solid nose 'Touch'.

out of shark mode. To begin, have some cookies available in a dish or in your pocket, and have a clicker in one hand. Form your empty hand into a loose fist, place the fist close to your puppy's nose and, as you do so, open your fingers so your palm is about a quarter inch from your puppy's nose. When you do this, your pup will most likely instinctively poke your palm with his nose to "smell" what you are doing. As the nose makes contact with your palm, click and give your puppy a cookie to reward his effort. Once again, place a loose fist right in front of and very close to the nose of your puppy and open your fingers to expose your palm. Click as your puppy noses your palm and reward. The first several repetitions should be done silently to avoid bombarding your pup with a word he doesn't know. As he figures out that nosing your palm is what gets clicked, start saying "Touch" just after the click and before the cookie. Begin switching hands and the orientation of your palm's angle so that your puppy doesn't make any superstitious assumptions. Pups quickly decide that perhaps only your right hand is the correct one or that your fingers must be pointing to the left. Changing it up early in the process prevents this. End the session when your puppy is engaged and successful. Always leave him wanting more.

The next time you play 'Touch', begin where you ended last time, with your palm still close to your puppy's nose and saying the word "Touch" just after the click. After a few repetitions, begin to place your palm a bit further from the pup's nose so he has to reach a bit to hit it. If he misses or doesn't try to reach and touch, do not click, do not say "Touch", and do not reward. Remove your palm and try again, this time closer to the nose to ensure success. Get a few more repetitions and then try again to add a bit of distance between your palm and the pup's nose. Once he does begin to reach to nose bop your palm, you can begin to say "Touch" as you open your fist and click when he makes contact. Saying the word prior to the click is the formation of a verbal cue, or asking for the behavior. Whenever a failure occurs, simply remove your palm without a click and do not reward. Next attempt, make it a bit easier to ensure success.

As your pup enjoys his new found talent, keep the game of 'Touch' interesting by adding more distance and changing the look of the game. At this point you can stop showing a closed fist and simply present an open palm. You can put your palm next to your puppy's head instead of in front of his nose. You can put your palm between your legs or behind your back. Make 'Touch' fun and challenging. As the puppy really seems to get it, stop clicking and rewarding every repetition (100% rate of reinforcement) and begin clicking and rewarding only some of the time (variable reinforcement). Eventually, if you make this game harder, just a speck at a time, you will be able to ask for 'Touch' when your dog is in another room or distant from you in your yard. A strong 'Touch' cue can even be used instead of 'Come'. I'll never forget a relieved and joyful telephone call I got from a client one day. She told me she had just started down the sidewalk with her leashed puppy and, somehow, the leash detached from his collar. She had no idea how this had happened, but her puppy, surprised as he was at his newfound freedom, started to run down the sidewalk away from her. We hadn't yet covered 'Come' in her lessons, but she had a really reliable 'Touch' on cue. Although in a state of panic over her puppy's safety, or lack thereof, she faked a cheerful tone of voice and yelled a happy "Touch" to her disappearing pup. Her pup stopped, turned around, and ran back to touch her palm with his nose. Whew, it really works! She scooped him up and ran back to her house. I think she stayed in for a month before she dared leave the doorstop again, but she knew she was well on her way to having a well-taught and safe dog.

You may now be wondering if 'Touch' has uses other than those already discussed. It sure does. Although we initially teach 'Touch' to stop your puppy from biting you, once the game is learned, don't hesitate to use it whenever it's helpful. There are several situations that come to mind:
- a close-up game to play in the waiting room at the vet
- a way to move your puppy out from in front of the cupboard when you are unloading groceries
- a way to exercise your puppy on rainy, icy or really hot days
- an outdoor game to teach your pup to pay attention in your yard or on walks
- a game to play just after answering your doorbell to keep your pup with you and not on your arriving guests

As you can see, your broad imagination and ability to 'think on your feet' really allow the uses for 'Touch' to be without limitation.

Give Me a 'Kiss'

If you don't want your puppy to think you are boring, it is a good idea to teach him multiple skills which can be used interchangeably and in similar situations. So, let's teach another replacement behavior for nipping, namely 'Kisses'.

When teaching your puppy to kiss or lick you, I suggest you di-

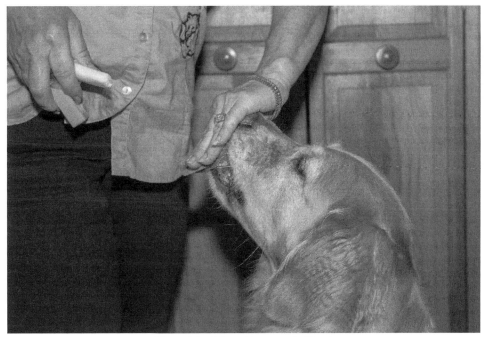
Glitter giving 'Kisses' to a scented hand.

rect his tongue to your fingertips and not your face. This doesn't mean you shouldn't allow your pup to lick your face, but only that the cue "Kisses" should be for fingers. When you teach the cue this way, you are able to increase its use and ask your pup to 'Kiss' people other than you. Some people don't want doggie licks on the face, but most people will allow fingertip kisses. If you cue fingers, you are safe. Whether to allow face licking is a personal choice and, since there are legitimate health reasons not to allow it, let's not put face licking on cue.

　　　To teach your puppy to lick your fingertips on cue is accomplished fairly quickly. Once taught, if a puppy begins to nip us, we can ask them for 'Kisses' instead. To begin this teaching, you need a smelly piece of food large enough to use as a sort of ink pad of scent and smaller pieces of food to use as your post-click reward. One hand will be your clicker hand and your reward hand, while your other hand will be the recipient of the kisses. It is important to keep these hands separate, although it is awkward at first. The reason for using a different hand to reward the pup, other than the one he kissed, is that we will initially scent the hand to be kissed to induce the behavior. We want to fade this food scent off the hand being kissed but if we use the same hand to reward, we are inadvertently re-scenting it every time we reward the pup. Let's begin and I think it will become easy to understand.

　　　Hold your clicker in one hand and rub your other empty hand on your large piece of food that is your scent pad. Offer the deliciously smelly fingertips to your puppy. When he licks due to the scent of the food, click with your clicker hand and then, also with your clicker hand, give the reward. Repeat by re-scenting your empty hand, offering it to your puppy, clicking when he licks and feeding a cookie using your clicker hand. Just as you did when teaching 'Touch', as your puppy figures out that it is his licking that is being clicked, begin to say "Kisses" just after you click. After a few more successful repetitions, offer your previously scented fingertips to your pup without re-scenting. If he licks, click and reward. If he doesn't lick when the scent is fading, remove your hand from in front of his face, re-scent, offer your smelly hand, click and say "Kisses" when he licks. Keep trying to get more than one incident of licking without re-scenting, or you will get stuck at the luring stage. You NEVER want to get stuck at the luring stage.

Play 'Kisses' often but not for more than five minutes or so at a time. Once you can get four or five repeated 'Kisses' without re-scenting your fingertips, you are on your way to having the behavior on cue. You can now start asking for a kiss as you extend your hand toward your pup, click for the lick and give a cookie. Next step, as you probably have guessed, is to begin your variable rate of reinforcement. Before you know it, no more scent is needed on your fingers and your pup will give you a kiss when you ask for one. At this point the behavior is reliable and you can use it as a replacement behavior for nipping. When your pup nips, ask for a kiss to get his tongue lick instead of his teeth. This game can be used interchangeably with the 'Touch' game, thus, offering an interesting change.

When you have 'Touch' and 'Kisses' on cue, you will find you will be using management techniques less. It is easier to say "Touch" than pull out a shield. It is more convenient to say "Kisses" than to crate your puppy or step over a baby gate. You need management techniques until the puppy is taught to do replacement behaviors. Once the teaching is complete, you don't need to manage as often. Won't it be nice to be rid of crates and gates? You are well on your way.

Chapter 8

An Open Door Is Not An Invitation

Rae's Doberman Tag protecting her home
at the open door.

Safety of your puppy is critical. A very common way puppies get into trouble is by not 'Waiting' when we need them to do so. Puppies move at the speed of light. I remember getting my first puppy when I was in my early twenties. I am not counting the dogs my parents owned, since I did little of the care and no one did any training!!! Once I was married and got a puppy, my husband and I were the "parents" and it was very different. That puppy was a Golden Retriever named Karat. She could move so fast from disaster to disaster that I felt she had somehow multiplied and I now had four or five puppies! I knew nothing about dog training or management. I would be cleaning up piddle, not realizing she was grabbing the edge of the tablecloth and was about to cause a dinner plate avalanche. When I was cleaning that up, she would be ripping up magazines I had left on the floor. It wasn't pretty. If only I had known then what I know now. 'Wait' would have been very high on the to-do list.

The behavior 'Wait' means 'Enter a holding pattern until I tell you it is time to act.' Yup, one little word means all that. An open crate door does not mean 'With me', an open front door does not mean 'Let's go', an open car door does not mean 'Get in' or 'Get out'. 'Wait' is so easy to teach there is no reason at all not to take the time to do so. An unfortunate memory is of one person who had booked her first puppy lesson with me, but before the lesson day came, the puppy ran out the front door and… I will spare you the details. The bottom line is that every puppy should know 'Wait'.

'Wait' in the Crate

The easiest way to begin teaching 'Wait' is with a crate, assuming you use one to contain your puppy at night and/or when you are not home or able to properly supervise. Pick a time when your puppy has been crated briefly or toss a cookie in the crate and close the door after the puppy runs in to eat it. As you put your hand on the latch to open the crate door, raise your other hand in front of the door and hold it with your palm flat, facing your puppy as if you were a policeman telling a pedestrian not to cross the street. Then, keeping your hand briefly in the 'Wait' position, say "Wait" and begin to unlatch the door, removing your 'Wait' signal hand. Whenever using a signal, never hold it too long or your hand becomes invisible like rain on a windshield. It is the motion of the signal that is meaningful to your puppy. As you begin to unlatch the door, give your 'Wait' signal again, say "Wait" and remove the hand signal. Continue to unlatch the door, little by little, saying "Wait" and signaling with your hand each time you move the latch. As you progress to actually opening the door, the pup will let you know how quickly to progress. As you say "Wait" and give the signal, if he comes toward the door as it opens, simply close the crate door and begin again. You are showing the puppy that staying in the crate causes the door to open and approaching the door causes it to close. Be gentle with the process to avoid catching a foot or nose in the crate door as you close it. If the puppy is fast and gets a foot, leg or snout out of the crate, gently replace the puppy with your hand, close the door and begin again. You may have noticed a clicker is not being used for this. The reason is you are not using food as the reward. The paycheck for 'Wait' is allowing the puppy to leave the crate when you give the release word. Since you are not using cookies, you don't use a clicker. Oh, while I am thinking of it, let me caution you about crate doors that have two latches instead of one: always fully fasten both latches. If you fasten only one of the latches, your puppy can push the door partially open and get a foot or a nose stuck when the door re-shuts. Not pretty. Now let's get back to teaching 'Wait'. Continue to slowly open the crate door as you repeat "Wait" both verbally and with your hand signal. If your puppy does 'Wait', you proceed. If your puppy pushes against the door, you close the door and try again. I find most puppies understand how to succeed in less than five minutes. Once you can completely open the door, say "Wait" one more time and then release your puppy to join you. Your release can either be what you say at the end of any exercise, such as 'Done', or you can use another phrase specifically when releasing 'Wait', such as 'Let's go' or 'With me'. The release should not be a big celebration but simply the end of the 'Wait'.

Once you begin to teach your puppy 'Wait' before exiting the crate, be certain to use it each and every time you open the crate door. If you find that first time out of the crate in the morning your puppy needs to pee too badly to make him 'Wait', abbreviate the entire process but still do a nanosecond of 'Wait' followed by your release. Consistency, consistency, consistency: puppies thrive on it.

'Wait' at the Door

Since puppies don't transfer behaviors from one location to another very effectively, let's help out by teaching your puppy that 'Wait' not only means 'Don't rush out of the crate', but also applies to the front door. Because the motivation here is safety and nothing else, have your pup

'Wait' before leaving your home but not necessarily before coming back in. Entering a building DOES become a safety issue away from home, however, such as the vet clinic or a pet store. You just never know when someone's dog may be at the end of a retractable leash and near the entrance while the owner is paying their bill or otherwise occupied. To avoid this canine greeting committee, who may or may not be good at their technique of saying "Hi", just avoid or manage the whole situation by asking your dog to "Wait" until you enter and then invite him to join

Andrew teaching Sadie 'Wait' at the door.

you. To teach 'Wait' at the door, whether exiting your home or entering another building where there are other dogs, follow the exact same steps

Riley learning 'Wait' in the crate.

Riley learning the release.

as waiting in the crate, using the house door as you did the crate door.

To begin, leash your puppy, go to the door and say "Wait" as you reach for the door knob. Since you don't have a third hand to give a stop sign signal, stepping toward the dog with one foot will keep him in place or even cause him to back up a bit as a response to the spatial pressure. Move your signal foot back next to your other foot and say "Wait" again as you proceed to open the door. Take note of your floor surface in the area of your doorway in order to come up with what your definition of success will be. For example, you may want your puppy to stay on the scatter rug in front of your door until you release. You may want your pup behind the metal threshold before you invite your puppy to join you. Whatever the detail, have criteria so you can be consistent with what you ask of your pup.

Because the price of door scooting is so high, I like to really push the envelope with teaching 'Wait' for this situation. Do not release your pup until the door is wide open and you are completely outside the door, standing on your porch or landing. Even then, repeat 'Wait' one more time before inviting your pup to join you with the same release word you used with 'Wait' in the crate. The entire process of getting out the door the first time takes less than five minutes to accomplish. I don't mean to imply that the behavior is solid in five minutes; far from it. You will, however, be astounded by the speed it does become well learned, simply because you can practice this each and every time you take your puppy out a door, any door.

Before we proceed to teaching 'Wait' for car doors, let's talk about a similar situation of 'Wait' at the front door with a slightly different twist. As your puppy ages, you will, most likely, be able to leave him home uncrated when you go out. It is equally, if not more important, your dog not scoot out as you leave without him, particularly since he won't be "dressed" in his leash. The only thing worse than a loose dog, is a loose, naked dog. To teach this behavior, leash the puppy and attach the handle to a heavy piece of furniture or a stair post in the entryway. Tell your pup to 'Wait' as you open the door, repeating the verbal cue as needed. As you step onto your porch, instead of releasing with "Let's go" or "With me" or something similar, say "I'll be back" or some such phrase of your liking. Shut the door between you and the puppy, wait a few seconds and then begin to open the door to re-enter. As you do so, the first word your puppy should hear is "Wait" since many pups scoot out the door not only when you are leaving but also when you are re-entering. Remember your pup is only tethered for the teaching process. All that is needed is to say "Wait", enter your home and then do whatever greeting you enjoy.

As a brief aside, you can also tell your pup "I'll be back" whenever you leave his presence throughout the day. Hearing this phrase begins to mean that you are leaving but there is absolutely no duration defined by the phrase. You may be leaving the room to get a glass of water, you may be leaving the house to get the mail out of the mailbox or you may be going to Madrid for a week. Hearing this phrase repeatedly becomes part of your dog's routine and he is not nervous about your departure. He realizes you always do return, although he doesn't know when that will be.

'Wait' in the Car

Just as with the front door, it's not a good idea for your puppy to jump out of your car without a cue to do so. My dogs are crated in my vehicle, but when I open the crates they must 'Wait' before jumping out. If crates are too big to put in your car, there are many seatbelt/harness options on the market. The rule is still the same though. 'Don't jump out of the car when I unclip your seatbelt harness. Wait'. As with the door at home, release your pup's 'Wait' by saying "With me" or your release phrase if the pup is joining you or "I'll be back" if he is waiting in the car. Only allow dogs to wait in the car in a safe area and when the temperature inside the car is not too hot or cold. For safety, I do not leave dogs in my car at a busy mall or in a parking spot that requires me to walk a long distance away. Also, air temperatures below 15 degrees F or above 60 degrees F can quickly become dangerous, too cold or too hot. Even leaving a car locked with a valet key with the air conditioning running doesn't help with a vehicle having a small engine or if the engine stalls and the AC stops working. Breeds vary in their tolerances so make sure you know what your breed can tolerate on both ends of the thermometer. Safety comes first, as always.

To begin transferring 'Wait' to the car situation, take your puppy for a car ride and use your arrival at home to begin. If your puppy rides loose in the car (not what I suggest, by the way), leash him before you exit the vehicle. Hold the leash as you open the door and begin saying "Wait" immediately. If the puppy tries to push past you to exit, stop and put your puppy back where he was before you began to open the door. Say "Wait" again and proceed to open your door. Since you have already familiarized your puppy with what 'Wait' means in different scenarios, he will begin to see you mean the same thing now. Repeat the word "Wait" and give your police officer hand signal as you proceed to open the door and exit the vehicle. Your puppy needs to 'Wait' until you release by saying "With me" or the release you use for exiting the crate and the front door of your home.

If your puppy does not ride loose in your car but is seat belted with a harness in the rear seat, the process is similar. Say "Wait" as you get out of the car. Close your door and open the back door where your puppy is secured. Say "Wait" as you attach the leash and unlatch the harness. Continue to say "Wait" until you are ready for your pup to exit and then say "With me" (or your release phrase).

'Wait' will be one of the most used behaviors you teach your puppy. It is a life-saving skill you can transfer to many different situations. If you have other people tell your puppy to 'Wait', they will learn to respect this cue from others. I'll never forget a summer party at my house and how handy this behavior was for my guests. My fenced yard has a gate to exit down to a lakefront. My dogs 'Wait' when I open this gate, even if they will be joining me for a swim. There is a sign on this gate asking people to tell my dogs to 'Wait' before opening the gate. I was sitting on the porch watching two teenage girls reading the sign and looking at each other and then at my two dogs. They were hesitant about opening the gate, doubting that their cue to 'Wait' would be successful. I encouraged them to go ahead and try it, so they did. My dogs stood there and watched them exit the gate, never moving a muscle. The high five which the girls victoriously shared, was a joy to behold. 'Wait' works!

Derek learning to teach Riley 'Wait' before leaving his open crate.

89

Chapter 9

Easy 'Come' / Easy Go

Mensa and Glitter coming on a hand signal.

Coming when called is a skill every dog should have and teaching this life-saving behavior while your dog is still a puppy is the easiest route for all involved. I bet you've heard the common expression "he follows me around like a puppy", which is common for a reason: it's true! Puppies, at least most puppies, tend to stay close to the humans in their family both inside the home and outside in the yard. As puppies mature, they begin to venture further as their view of what is safe expands. Breeders have told me they can go for a walk with their older dogs, never closing the gate behind them for very young puppies. Going beyond the gate is not viewed as "safe" to the pups and they will not follow. Once the pups are a couple of months old, however, the gate must be shut as they are gaining confidence and can't be trusted to stay behind an open gate. To avoid losing your brave little pup, let's begin to teach your puppy to come when called, first time, every time.

'Come' When You Want To (Motivational Recall)

It is always wise to fully decide what you mean by a word before you begin to teach it to your puppy and the word 'Come' is no exception. My definition of 'Come' is "I need to put my hand in your collar, I can't reach you, I am not going to move, you have two seconds to get to me and I will only say 'Come' once." Yup, one little word can say all of that to your pup when you teach him exactly what you want.

When teaching 'Come', what gets clicked is putting your hand in your pup's collar. When a puppy is called, if you aren't able to get him by the collar, a couple of different things can happen, neither of which is good! He might run to you faster than the speed of light, grab the cookie from you and keep on going, also at the speed of light. I call this type of recall the "drive-by recall" since he is still a long way from you but in the opposite direction from where he started. Another possibility is that your pup will run right at you until he is just out of reach, avoid getting any closer to you and not let you get any closer to him. I call this type of recall the "hockey goalie recall" since that is what your pup resembles as he moves from side to side avoiding your reach. Let's avoid both scenarios and teach him from the beginning that offering his collar is part of 'Come'.

Let's begin by making 'Come' the most fun game your pup has ever played. Ironically, making your pup want to come is accomplished by letting him think we are not going to let him do so: sort of reverse psychology, I guess. This method is a restrained recall, since we will need a

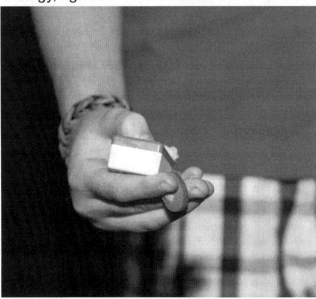

person to literally restrain your puppy until you call him, while you are tempting him with cookies and running away from him. It's a good idea to practice the last step first, since it is sure to be a bit awkward if you try it for the first time while your puppy is running at you a hundred miles an hour. Here is what the very end of your 'Come' will look like: you have a clicker in your hand, thumb resting on the trigger and a large,

Holding the lure and the clicker in the same hand for 'Come'.

clearly visible reward or a long, shoestring shaped cookie in the same hand, held dangling between your index and middle finger. String cheese works well for this or any meat you can cut into skinny strips. Show the dangling cookie to your puppy and, as he reaches for it, slide your empty hand UNDER your clicker hand and take hold of your pup's collar under his chin. If you reach over his head to take his collar he will shrink away from you since most puppies are instinctively head shy. Once your hand is in the collar (your pup is still sniffing at the cookie), click and give your puppy the cookie from between your fingers. If you think that the click will bother him close to his face, simply move your clicker hand and the cookie away from his face while you click. While you are rewarding your puppy with the meat or cheese, praise him while your hand is still in his collar. As you remove your hand from the collar, say your release word. Now that the end is clear, let's go back to the beginning of the game.

Step 1: Find a place in your house where you have a straight path for eight to ten yards. This path will serve as a runway to teach your pup to come. It is best if you can create several areas to practice helping the pup generalize his learning. Some runways can be shorter than others, some can involve going around furniture, but, initially, you need to be able to see your puppy when you call him. Have someone hold your puppy at one end of the runway, one hand in the collar and the other hand in front of his chest holding him back. Hold your clicker and cookie in one hand as described above and begin to tease your puppy as your partner holds the puppy back. Run away, teasing and acting like you are a bunny being pursued by a greyhound until you are several yards back from your pup, at the end of the runway. In the most enthusiastic voice you can muster, say your puppy's name followed by the word "Come". This is your partner's cue to let go of the puppy. Your tone of voice should imply that you are inviting your puppy to the best party on earth. Dogs are very sensitive to tone of voice and a playful, enthusiastic tone is what we are going for. This restrained recall will cause your puppy to fly to you like a cannonball out of a cannon for several reasons:
- the puppy is being restrained like a racehorse behind a starting gate
- you are dangling a tasty cookie in front of his face
- you take off running bringing out the chase instinct in your pup
- you call with the enthusiasm of a motivational speaker

When your puppy arrives, you know what to do: lure him close to you with the cookie in your clicker hand, slip your empty hand into his collar under his chin (not over his head), click, give him the cookie while you

Andrew restrains Sadie as Ryan begins to tease and lure for 'Come'.

Sadie getting ready to run to Ryan as he backs away.

praise and release him with your 'Done' word as you let go of his collar. Repeat this process three or four more times, always varying where the puppy is restrained in your home and where you stand when you say his name followed by "Come". Be sure you are within the line of vision since we are luring with a visible cookie which is only visible if he can see you as you call him. Do three or four sessions per day, for three or four days. Then you're ready to move on to step two. Have I mentioned there are eight steps? Don't worry, you're well on your way.

Step 2: Step two is identical to step one with one variation: instead of teasing your pup right in front of his face, start a few feet away from where he is being restrained, about one third of the way down your runway. This seemingly small change increases the difficulty in two ways: you have the delectable cookie further from his nose and you have less distance to run away in prey-mode. Your puppy will still run to you as fast as he can since that is what you taught him to do in step one. Repeat step two as you did step one: three or four times for a session, three or four sessions per day, for three or four days. Now you can move on to step three.

Step 3: Step three is identical to steps one and two except you start teasing even further from your puppy, two thirds of the way down your runway, giving you less distance to run like a bunny. Everything else is the same and then, a few days later, on to step four.

Step 4: Step four is identical to steps one, two and three except that you start teasing from where you will be standing when you call him, at the end of your runway. There is no more running to incite prey drive. Just say his name playfully and enthusiastically and give the cue "Come". Lickety split, he arrives in a flash. Repeat step four just as you did the first three steps. Ready??? A big change is brewing in step five.

Ryan goes further down the runway as Andrew continues to restrain.

Step 5: Step five is the end of luring and teasing with a visible cookie. For this stage of training, have the cookies available in your pocket or in a dish you can reach when you call your puppy. Because removal of the lure is such a jump in difficulty, let's make it easier in some other way.

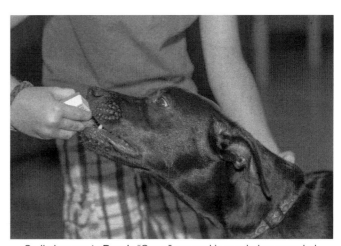

Sadie has run to Ryan's "Come" cue and is now being rewarded.

Guess how we can do that? Instead of calling the puppy from a stationery endpoint as in step four, let's go closer to the pup as in step two so that we can run away and create the prey drive for him to chase us. There is no point in going back in his face as we did in step one since then we would be advertising the fact the cookie is no longer visible. Start a few feet from your pup, talk and tease with facial expressions and playful behavior, run away, turn and face your restrained puppy and say his name followed by "Come". When he arrives, slip your free hand under his chin into his collar and click with your clicker hand. Then, guess what, the cookie magically appears from your pocket or the nearby dish. You are saying to your pup, "See that? I DID have a cookie even though you couldn't see it. Life is good when you come to me". Stick with step five the same way you did

95

the others: three or four times for each session, three or four sessions per day for three or four days. Since there is no longer a visible lure, you can now go out of sight before you call your pup. You can go around a corner, into another room, or to the second floor of your house if your pup is held downstairs and vice versa.

Step 6: Step six moves you back further from where the pup is restrained, similar to where you teased for step three (two thirds of the way down your runway), run away and call.

Step 7: Step seven starts where step four started (end of the runway), many yards from the restrained dog and no running back and teasing. All of this may seem repetitive, which is by design. When your puppy hears his name followed by "Come", we want him to stop what he is doing and run to you. There should be no decision making involved. He should come, first time, every time. His response could literally determine life or death.

'Come' When You Don't Want To (Distracted Recall)

Step 8: So far, we have made it fairly easy for your puppy to come when called. You are fun and there's not much else going on so there's really little reason not to come to you. Also you have done all seven steps in the house, with little distraction. In step eight you will begin to add distraction while still in the house but in a way that will teach your puppy he can come to you even when he is tempted by another option.

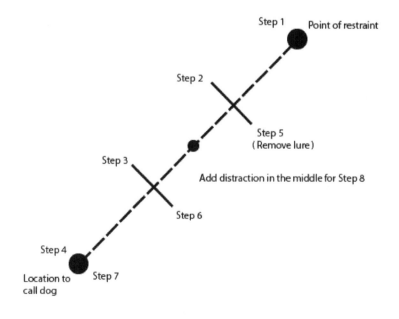

In the beginning it is important you choose a distraction you can control. If you have a third person available to help, that makes this pretty doable. I use this third person as a sort of 'monkey in the middle' arming him with a bag of cookies or an irresistible toy and placing him halfway down our recall runway. The person should be standing up, holding a sealed bag of cookies or a toy that is partially concealed in his hands. You should say the pup's name a couple of times in an enthusiastic tone of voice and then say "Come". The pup will most likely run right past the person holding the distraction to get to you and he should then be rewarded for doing so just as we did in step seven. Each repetition should get ever so slightly more difficult by making the cookies or the toy more tempting. If using cookies, next time have the bag open but still held up at the chest level of the person holding it. Next, the distractor can rattle the open bag. Next, the person can bend down, holding the bag lower and more at dog level. Next, he can dump some cookies on the floor, but partially cover them with a hand. Next, he can expose the dumped cookies. After you call the dog, if you see any hesitation in the pup as he nears the distraction, playfully say his name again or even repeat "Come" to remind him what he is doing.

As you increase temptation, your pup may falter long enough that he starts to think going after the cookies or toy on the floor may be the way he wants to go. If that happens, we need to have a plan in place to convince the puppy to make the right choice. As he stops running to you and approaches the cookie decoy, the protector of the distraction should make those cookies unavailable to the pup. Now approach the puppy as he lingers near the unavailable distraction and, upon arrival, remove the hidden reward cookies from your pocket and show them to the puppy, making sure he can't reach them. Taunt him with the reward and then run back to where you were when you said "Come" and call him again, even if he is following you. Upon his arrival, place your hand in his collar and reward him. What we have done is stop his behavior of going to the distraction. There is no pain or fear involved, but it is still effective. After his difficulty, set up another recall, making the distraction just slightly less appealing than the time he failed. He will, most likely, run right past the distraction since last time going to the cookies or toy on the floor didn't prove successful for him. When the puppy gets to you, reward him lavishly. Continue to make the distraction more and more difficult, responding as described above for any failure to pass by the distraction. After he learns the distraction is not for him, don't be surprised if your puppy tries to avoid going near it as he runs to you. I have seen dogs run in a huge curve and even go to the other side of furniture next to the runway to avoid being tempted. My most vivid memory of this phenomenon was when I was working with a couple and their dog in the game room of their home. There was a runway next to their pool table and we were using hotdogs on the floor as the distraction which I was guarding with my life. When the pup came to the smell of the hot dogs, I protected them so he couldn't indulge. The owner came to us, showed the pup the steak in his pocket without giving him any and ran back to where he had called him. When he said "Come", the pup ran to him and got the steak. We set up another repetition using the same runway. This time the puppy avoided the hot-dogs by going all the way around the pool table! This avoidance of the distraction shows great learning. We rejoiced.

Once you have completed all eight steps in the house, three or four days per step, it is time to take the show on the road, or at least out in the yard. Make sure your puppy is safe by working either in a fenced area or having one hundred feet of quarter inch diameter rope on your pup as a drag line which can be stepped on if needed. Begin with step one and work your way through all eight steps again, this time doing two or three days per step. When you get to step eight, you can use the yard itself as a distraction. Bring your puppy outside and let him sniff around the yard. When he starts to get interested in whatever he has found, call him to you. If he doesn't come immediately, go to him, show him the reward you were going to give him, run away and call him again. Have a big reward party when he comes and let him go sniffing again. Keep working this using the actual environment as the distraction until his ability to come to you, no matter what, is in place.

Practicing Alone

All of the training we have discussed so far requires more than one person; two people for the restrained recall and three people for the distracted recall. You may not always have the luxury of having someone to help you, so we need a way to practice when you are alone. To accomplish this, we are going to use a slight deviation of 'Find It' which we discussed in Chapter 6. As a quick refresher, 'Find It' involves showing a cookie to your pup, saying "Find It" and then tossing the cookie away from your pup. He runs to get it and automatically looks back at you to see if you are going to throw another. His looking back at you is what we clicked in this game. In order to use this game to teach 'Come', we will change it slightly. Show your puppy the cookie, say "Find It" and throw the cookie.

He will run to the cookie and eat it and as he looks back at you, instead of clicking, start running away from him. This will cause him to chase you. As he does so, say his name and "Come", capturing the act of him running toward you. When he gets to you, lure him close with a second cookie between the fingers of your clicker hand, place your free hand in his collar, click, praise and release. Although this method is not as effective as the restrained recall with two people, it serves as a nice supplement when you are by yourself.

When you are working the distracted recall, a third person to control the bag of cookies or the toy is a real luxury. Instead of using a person, you can protect the distraction by making it unavailable to your puppy in a different way. All you need to accomplish this is a sturdy container that allows the scent of the cookies or the sight of the toy to be obvious to your puppy while, at the same time, preventing the puppy from getting to the cookies or the toy. Readymade items can be used such as glass jars with perforated screw tops in the form of salt shakers or parmesan cheese dispensers. If you want to make your own, you can use empty plastic jars and lids, such as peanut butter jars, with holes drilled in the plastic lids. Larger containers can be used for toys, such as clear plastic storage containers. These containers may lure your dog to the distraction but prevent him from indulging while you go to him to tease him with the vision of your reward cookies. See what I mean? You can begin with food that only has a slight scent in the beginning and then work up to very smelly food such as tuna or pepperoni. You can use food in the jar that you wouldn't want to feed to your puppy since he won't ever eat what is in the jar, but will always be rewarded with the cookies in your pocket.

If you see teaching 'Come' as a real project, you are correct. This is a commitment of several weeks of daily training, but the end product could save the life of your dog several times over the next twelve to fifteen years. Whether you plan to let your dog run free in selected areas or never plan to do so, every dog should know how to come when called. Mechanical failure could always rear its ugly head. Just today I heard from a new client whose dog was safely harnessed and leashed while on a walk. As the owner bent down to make good use of his poop bag, somehow the leash came unattached from the harness and the dog was loose on a busy road. This nasty case of mechanical failure ended with the dog hospitalized for several days after being struck by a car. A reliable recall could have saved the dog and owner a lot of anguish. Three weeks of training beats even three days in the veterinary hospital.

Chapter 10

Assume Your Position

Glitter in a 'Down' and Mensa in a 'Sit'.

As your puppy continues to grow and mature into a loving and well behaved member of your family, it is frequently convenient to be able to
ask him to be in a specific position. Different situations and activities
may require that your pup be sitting or standing or perhaps lying down.
Once taught with our now familiar win/win style, your canine companion will be happy to oblige.

'Sit' is frequently the first position most dog owners teach their puppies. Luring, having the dog follow a visible treat, is the simplest way to begin. Many times when I ask a dog owner if their pup sits on cue, the response is, "Oh yes he does, but only if I am holding a cookie." My reaction to this is the pup is not really trained to 'Sit' on cue but simply has been taught to eat in a seated position! This phenomenon is common and is the biggest downfall of luring: the pup can't 'Sit' if the human doesn't have a cookie and the human can't bring themselves to ask unless waving a piece of roast beef over the dog's nose. Luring can go wrong in this way because dogs are such detailed thinkers (remember they are little lawyers) the cookie in the hand actually becomes a part of the signal the dog understands. Remove the cookie, the signal is incomplete. In addition to the cookie being a part of the signal, luring can quickly turn into bribing, which is not a good thing. Instead, we want to go from luring to rewarding, which IS a good thing.

To begin properly teaching 'Sit', show your pup a treat very close to and slightly above his nose. Keep the treat within smelling distance and slowly move your morsel back, heading for the top of the pup's head,

making sure his nose follows the scent. Begin to arch the cookie down toward his head so as his nose goes up toward the cookie, his butt goes down toward the floor. As soon as his cute little bottom hits the floor, click and give him the cookie you used as a lure, simultaneously saying "Sit" to announce what he has done. Slowly repeat the

Lorin rewarding Kendall after clicking 'Sit'.

word "Sit" a few times, teaching him this is the word associated with his newly assumed position. Don't confuse this repetitive language with the faulty practice of asking multiple times that your dog do something. Giving your dog multiple cues teaches the dog they don't have to do it the first time you say it since you just keep saying it until they do it. By repeating "Sit" <u>after</u> he sits, we are teaching language, not repeating a cue. When you are finished rewarding your pup, but before he gets up, give him his 'Done' release word as you have with previous behaviors. At first you simply want to beat him to the punch and say "Done" before he pops up. As this routine is practiced, he will begin to realize he hears that word before moving and will learn that he is not supposed to move until he hears it.

Sometimes a pup will be quicker than we are and stand up when we click. Technically he is correct, since the click marks and therefore ends the behavior. If, after you click, your pup pops into a stand, simply use the cookie in your hand you haven't yet given him, to raise his nose and again lower his butt to the floor. Do not click again since you owe him for the first click. Instead, reward and release. In order to prevent the popping up behavior, simply continue to say "Sit" after he sits, which lets him know to stay in position until you release with "Done". You'll find this termination word very handy once you fade out the clicker and cookies to let your pup know for sure when 'Sit' is over.

After you say "Done" and your pup gets up, walk to a new location in the room and repeat the lured sit. Click, reward and release as above. Move to a third spot in the room and repeat again. This time after you say "Done" and he stands up, place your hand over the his nose as if you had a cookie and most likely he will sit since he has learned already that this hand motion is a signal to 'Sit'. When he does, click and give him a jackpot of several small treats one at a time from your pocket as you comment on his position by repeating "Sit" and then release. You have just avoided the pitfall of a cookie remaining part of your hand signal and you moved from luring to rewarding within four repetitions of the behavior. Good job. Feel free to end your session with this success. Let your pup rest and/or play for at least an hour or two before doing your next 'Sit' lesson. When you are both ready to resume, go to a different room of your house to teach your pup that 'Sit' has the same meaning in a different location. Although this may seem obvious to you, your pup does not translocate cues when they are first learning them. Because you have changed locations, begin this session with a lured 'Sit', but after you release, go to a cookie-free signal, rewarding after the click when he sits. Move around this new room, repeating your 'Sit' signal, clicking, rewarding and releasing.

After a few rooms of your house have been added to your collection of 'Sit' locations, it is time to begin using 'Sit' as a cue, rather than a commentary on what your puppy has already accomplished. The universal method of switching any hand signal to a verbal cue is quite simple. Look at your standing puppy, say "Sit", and when he gives you a blank stare as if to ask "What does that mean?", give him his 'Sit' hand signal to define the word you just said. As you raise your hand over his head, he will sit and you can click and reward him for his efforts. Release, look at him and say "Sit". If he is still lacking in his language translation, define the word with your hand signal, click and reward. Repeat this scenario until, lo and behold, you say "Sit" and his little bottom hits the deck. Celebrate his success with a click and a jackpot. Now you have 'Sit' on either a verbal cue or a hand signal. Having both methods to communicate with your pup will come in handy. For example, a verbal cue is convenient when your hands are full, but a hand signal is useful if you want to ask your pup to do something when you are talking to someone else.

As soon as you have your 'Sit' behavior in place, it is time to begin fading out the click and the cookie. Begin this by clicking and giving a cookie for most 'Sits', but slipping in some that are not clicked or rewarded with food but simply praised and released. Over a few days, slip in more and more praise-only repetitions until, over a week or so, very rarely will you be commenting on a successful 'Sit' with a click. You can always return to a more frequent rate of reinforcement when you are in a distracting environment or when you are outside. This will help your puppy learn to listen to you even when there is a lot of activity competing for his attention. Now, on to the more relaxed position of 'Curl'.

'Curl'

There will many times when you want to ask your puppy to lie down, either on his bed or elsewhere. A few examples that come to mind are your meal times, family movie night, car rides, vet visits or when you stop on the sidewalk to talk with a neighbor. You may choose any word as your cue for this, but my preference is 'Curl' since I want my pup relaxed when he lays down, curled over on one hip with both hind feet on the same side of his body. To begin, have your puppy seated at your side, facing the same direction as you. Have a cookie in your hand, the right hand if your pup is seated to your left and your left hand if he is seated to your right. Show your pup the cookie in front of his nose and, keeping it close so he can smell it, lower it slowly toward the floor causing him to dip his shoulders and then drop his elbows and chest onto the floor. Once he is down, prior to giving him the cookie, curve the cookie around his face toward his ear, the one closest to you. As your puppy's head curves around toward you, he will flop over onto his hip, into the 'Curl' position I described above. This hip flop is when you click, give him the cookie and say your 'Curl' word followed by a release. Repeat this process a few times in various parts of the room you are in, and end the session. You will progress with 'Curl' exactly as you did with 'Sit'. Vary the location, fade out the lure and then use 'Curl' as a cue before the behavior. Your puppy is learning what you want as you move the signal in this downward curl around his head. Once he seems solid, teach him the verbal cue only, just as you did with 'Sit', by saying "Curl" and delaying the signal you have taught him. Soon he will 'Curl' on the verbal or the signal so you can begin fading the click and the cookie and off you go. A word of caution is in order here: never try to get your puppy to lie in a position you have never seen him assume on his own. Watch your puppy when he curls up to take a nap, and notice if he flops over on either hip or if he is always on the same hip. If he shows a definite preference, honor that. A puppy's hip structure is not always the same on both sides, which can cause a pref-

erence in 'Curl' direction. Be aware, it is easier to flop him on his left hip if you start with him seated on your left so you can curve his head to the right. If he prefers to rest on his right hip, teach him the 'Curl' cue with him seated on your right, curving his head around to his left. If he can go either way, teach both.

Rob luring Sadie into a 'Down'.

'Down'

'Down' is the word I use to describe the position when a pup lies flat on the floor with his haunches down but with one rear leg on each side of his body, in a sort of sphinx position or that of a lion ready to pounce on prey. To a detailed thinking dog, this sort of 'Down' is a totally different body position than the 'Curl', and it is taught in a completely different way.

This position may be used in place of the 'Curl' for a dog who doesn't want to flop on either hip but rather sleeps on his own in this sphinx pose. It can also be used to quickly down your puppy in an emergency situation.

Instead of beginning with your pup seated at your side, teach 'Down' to your pup when he is standing facing you. Put a cookie in front of his nose and lower it to the ground so, as he follows the smell of the cookie, his front end begins to lower into a bow position (elbows on the ground and cute little butt in the air). When the elbows hit, push the cookie at floor level toward the puppy's chest between his front legs causing him to lower his hips to the ground. When contact with the floor is complete, click and reward as you say "Down" and release when you are ready for him to get up. Proceed as above for 'Sit' and 'Curl', always using your luring motion as your signal, then switching to a verbal and then, finally, fading out the click and the reward. Now, let's go on to 'Stand'.

'Stand'

So far you have learned to teach your pup to 'Sit', 'Curl', and 'Down'; in other words, not to 'Stand'. There are times you will want your pup to be standing, such as when you need to put on a harness, trim his back toenails, or have him move out of your way when you're cooking or cleaning. There are two different ways to teach 'Stand' from a 'Sit' depending on the end product you want. With the first, the dog rises and moves forward, while with the second, he rises and stays in place. If you select the first, simply put a cookie in front of his nose while he's seated at your side, move the cookie away from the puppy at nose level, and he will stand so he can reach it. Click when he does so, saying "Stand", give him the cookie and release. This type of 'Stand', although easy to teach, causes the dog to move from the place he was seated, which I personally dislike. If you want your dog to be able to 'Stand' and end up in the same place he was sitting, you may want to consider the second method. This is convenient on the vet exam table or scale, when you are in a crowded area or when he is on a grooming table. Although it takes a little longer to teach this stationary stand, it is the one you may find more useful. Start with your pup in a 'Sit' at your side. Put a cookie in front of his nose but, instead of moving it forward for the pup to follow, curve the cookie down around his mouth toward his throat where the human 'Adam's apple' is located. As your puppy cocks his head down to follow the cookie, his rear end will pop up into a stand. As this happens, click, reward as you say 'Stand' and release. It may take several attempts to get the first 'Kickback Stand', but he will eventually be successful. If he just doesn't get it after five minutes of trying, release him from the sit, and ask him to do something he knows well so he can earn that cookie you have been using to lure. Let him rest for an hour or more and try again. A dog is able to learn anything you have the patience to teach as long as the behavior doesn't require opposable thumbs! Just stick with it.

Now that you know how to teach all four body positions, you may wonder if you should teach them in any certain order and whether to do them concurrently or one at a time.   The order really makes no difference. Teach whichever you have the greatest need for your puppy to know. You can also teach them all to the puppy at the same time, and even in the same session. Dogs are such detailed thinkers that any confusion they show rapidly vanishes. The biggest mistake I see people making is not challenging their pups enough, rather than too much. Let me remind you that dogs can be taught to lead blind people through busy intersections. I bet learning 'Down' and 'Sit' at the same time is not too much for them. However, one way the detailed brain in our pups CAN get confused is if you teach 'Sit' from a 'Stand', as we did, and then expect him to know what to do if you ask him to 'Sit' from a 'Down' or a 'Curl'. He will look at you as if he has never heard the word 'Sit' before. You can certainly teach him to 'Sit' from a 'Down' or a 'Curl' but it must be taught with a lure, just as we taught him to 'Sit' from a 'Stand'. You can still use the word 'Sit' however, since the final body position is exactly the same in the end. The same is true for 'Stand' from a 'Down' or a 'Curl' if you taught it originally from a 'Sit'. Just think like a dog, your narcissistic lawyer with ADHD, and you'll be all set.

Chapter 11

Only Breathe, Blink and Swallow
(In Other Words 'Stay')

Glitter on a 'Curl' / 'Stay' and Mensa on a 'Down' / 'Stay'.

When a dog is asked to 'Stay', he should do exactly that. The word 'Stay' instructs the pup to remain in the body position he has assumed, not to move from the location, even an inch, not to wag his tail or indulge in body hygiene, but he may breathe, blink and swallow. That's a lot to ask of a dog. In fact, 'Stay' is the most difficult of all behaviors to teach. Dogs find 'Stay' so difficult to learn because it is hard to explain to them that 'Stay' is different from doing nothing: it is a task. This was made really clear to me when watching street performers in Las Vegas who paint themselves all one color to look like a statue, assume a position, and don't move... at all... ever. Their buckets fill with tips as they perform by doing what appears to be nothing: not easy for human or canine.
  Ready? Let's teach this difficult skill to your perpetual motion puppy.

'Stay' and Duration

The key to all teaching is to break down the task at hand into easily learned chunks. For 'Stay' this must be done with both duration of the behavior and the distance you want to be able to go from your puppy when he is in a 'Stay'. Teaching duration is first, since we need some duration in place in order to move away from and return to the pup without him moving. Teaching a pup to 'Stay' should begin with the duration he can attain successfully, namely a nanosecond. Ask your pup to assume one of the positions you have taught him: a 'Sit', a 'Curl', a 'Down' or a 'Stand'. It usually isn't necessary to teach 'Stay' in both the 'Curl and the 'Down' but only in the one your puppy usually chooses on his own when he plunks down for a rest. Once your pup is at your side and in the position you requested, say "Stay" and put a stop sign hand signal briefly in front of his face. Immediately click, reward from your pocket and use your release word to end the 'Stay'. Move to a new spot in the room and repeat. You can do the entire session with the same body position in different locations, but it is also okay to change the pup's position for each repetition within a session. 'Stay' means 'Stay' in whichever position the pup is in. After a few minutes, no more than five, end the session.

The next time you practice 'Stay' increase the duration ever so slightly, from a nanosecond to a full second. In the next session increase to three seconds. As you are increasing your duration, it is fine to repeat the word 'Stay' as your puppy is doing so. This is just a reminder of what he is doing, and to continue until he hears the click, is rewarded and released. Once you have a solid ten seconds, begin to yoyo your duration so your pup doesn't see 'Stay' getting harder and harder each session. Teaching duration in a linear fashion can be discouraging and your pup starts to think you may be planning to have him do a 'Stay' while you go off to Bermuda for a week! If you throw in your occasional nanosecond 'Stay', your pup is less likely to get anxious about what you have in mind for the future of this behavior. Build, in this "peak and valley" fashion, until you have thirty seconds of duration.

'Stay' and Distance

All of the above have been done with the pup at your side.   Neither of you has moved even an inch and you are up to thirty seconds of duration. It is now time to start building distance from your stationary pup. To begin, ask your pup to 'Sit', 'Down', 'Curl', or 'Stand', and give

Glitter and Mensa on a 'Stay' cue in the 'Sit' Position.

your concurrent verbal and hand signal 'Stay'. Immediately pivot in front of your puppy, facing him, and repeat your verbal and hand signal, 'Stay'. As soon as you have done that, click, reward, and release. You have changed what you are doing by moving from the pup's side to facing him so drop your duration back to a nanosecond. With each repetition, increase the duration spent facing your puppy until you have ten seconds of duration. Begin to yoyo your duration, slowly working your way up to thirty seconds, just as you did when you were beside your puppy.

Once you are up to thirty seconds of duration, you can add one step of distance from your pup. Have your pup assume a position at your side, say and signal "Stay" but instead of pivoting, take one step straight forward and then pivot and face your pup. After a nanosecond, click where you are, re-cue the "Stay", and return to the puppy to reward and release. Build up to thirty seconds of duration, repeating "Stay" as needed. Now go two steps away, but only for a nanosecond. Continue building distance in small increments until you are as far as you ever expect to want to go (this can include out of the line of vision). Notice when you leave your pup's side, you walk away and don't back away. If you face your puppy and back away, your body language is actually saying "Come" while your mouth is saying "Stay". A puppy will just hate that incongruity. He wants us to say what we mean with both our body and our words. The two should match or you will have one confused puppy. Always click when you are at the maximum distance away for that repetition since that is what you want to mark with the click. Re-cue the "Stay" after the click, so your pup knows to wait for your return and his reward.

'Stay' Issues

You may be questioning why we have not addressed what to do if your puppy gets out of position during a 'Stay'. The reason is so simple that you will be surprised. We have broken the 'Stay' into such teeny-tiny pieces your puppy is likely to never have an issue. Our criteria for success has been increased so slowly the pup just goes with the flow, or, in this case, doesn't go anywhere! If, however, something does cause a break in a stay, it is usually after you have built quite a bit of duration and distance. If this happens, the less you react the better. If your pup lays down while in a 'Sit', 'Stay', simply slowly walk toward the pup, staring at the floor right in front of his paws. As you get closer, the special pressure he feels from your impending arrival will cause him to sit back up, without you saying a word. When he does so, tell him to 'Stay' and leave again. If your puppy sits up from a 'Down', which is less likely than going 'Down'

Lucia's Bella, Mike's Inky, Janet's Toby, and Kathleen's Catie
doing a 'Stay' in a 'Sit' position in obedience class.

from a 'Sit', go back to him expressionless, and tell him to 'Down', 'Stay' and leave again. If he moves from his location, walk toward the location he vacated, leading him back there by pointing your finger at his destination, ask him to assume his previous position, 'Stay' and leave. After you have once again resumed the 'Stay', don't wait too long before clicking, re-cuing and returning to reward. You want success to follow the mistake.

Whew! Bet you're glad this chapter is over. Me, too. Teaching your puppy to 'Stay' is a lot of work. If you don't see a useful application, it is fine to not teach 'Stay' at all. As long as your puppy knows 'Wait' so he is not door or vehicle scooting without permission, it is quite possible that he can lead a safe and happy life without 'Stay'. In fact, I have never once told one of my own dogs to "Stay" in the home situation but they'll 'Wait' 'til the cows come home.

Chapter 12

World's Most Rhetorical Question: Wanna Go For A Walk?

Ginny very excited about Adam putting her harness on
her. Photo by Aurora Young

Before you venture out for a walk with your new furry friend, there are some decisions to be made. Where will you go for a walk? How far will you walk? What equipment will you be using? What will you do if your pup pulls you forward or refuses to move? Where do you want your pup to walk in relation to you? What will you do if you meet another dog during your walk? With all of these decisions, are you now too tired to go? It's best to consider all of the above prior to hitting the road or you may find yourself in a bit of a predicament.

Walking Basics

Where you walk your pup is an easy choice for some people given where they live, but can be an issue for others. If you live in a neighborhood with lots of houses and sidewalks, you can pretty much step out your door and begin your adventure. However, if you live on a major road with fast moving traffic and no sidewalks, you will need to find a safer walking environment. Cars whizzing by can scare your puppy and make walking stressful instead of fun-filled. The walking surface is important. If you have access to a non-paved area, that's great. However, if you only have access to asphalt, you will want to consider including softer ground in your walks, at least a portion of the time. An unforgiving walking surface can be tough on your puppy's open growth plates and joints. Bone and joint development should also be considered when deciding how far to walk with a young pup. Cut your walks short until your pup is a year to a year and a half old. Allowing your pup to meander rather than power walk is important. Don't expect a four month old to train for a marathon with you. Build up distance slowly, allow the pup to self-regulate speed and allow him to stop and rest if he seems tired. Going for a walk shouldn't be so long as to cause your pup to be tired the rest of the day or, heaven forbid, limping. Extended lethargy or limping is a reason to visit your vet. Don't get off on the wrong foot with walks that are too long, too fast or totally on a hard surface.

Choosing a Collar

If you will be using a collar on your pup, there is a lot to consider. You can find collars in many different materials including fabric, leather and chain. Most collars are adjustable so you don't need to buy a new one once a week, which is how fast it seems some pups grow! Proper fit is essential, and should be checked often as your pup increases in size. You should always be able to easily get one or two fingers under the collar or it is too tight. You should never be able to pull the collar over one ear of your pup, or he could back out of it at the worst possible time and escape from the safety of your presence. Not too tight and not too loose are essential when it comes to collars. Once your pup is in a collar that will fit for life, you can choose one that has an identification plate attached or has a name and phone number woven into the fabric. Tags with this information are also available, but hanging one from your pup's collar poses the risk of it getting caught which can be problematic.

A collar that can cause some confusion is called a Martingale collar. This collar has an extra loop of material where the leash attachment occurs. The construction of this collar has a very specific use: dogs with narrow heads can easily slip out of regular collars unless the adjustment is tighter than is comfortable. The Martingale's extra loop of material allows the collar to relax a bit and loosen around the neck unless there is a leash

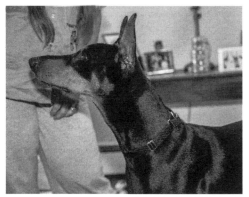

Tag in a relaxed martingale collar.

Proper adjustment so Tag won't choke when a leash is attached to the martingale.

attached to keep the collar tight. The adjustment is very precise on the Martingale collar: when a leash is attached and the collar is as tight as it can be, it should not be able to tighten to a size SMALLER than the circumference of the pup's neck. If a Martingale collar is adjusted too small, it will actually act as a choke collar although that is not the intent of the design.

Training using force free methods requires no use of a choke chain or a prong (pinch) collar. These devices are reserved for training that employs pain and fear to force compliance which is the opposite of the training philosophy we are using.

Choosing A Leash

It never ceases to amaze me what a large assortment of choices are available for the simplest of things. Buy salad dressing lately? I am tempted to go back to oil and vinegar for my salads to avoid the mile long aisle I have to traverse to find what I want in a dressing. Buy a leash lately? There are six foot leashes, four foot leashes, fifteen foot leashes, leashes with two handles, leather leashes, nylon leashes, chain leashes (good for leash chewing puppies), retractable leashes, wide leashes, narrow leashes and a rainbow of colors from which to choose. What you buy should have thought behind it, not just an appealing price or the first one you find on the rack.

Length depends on where you will be walking and how far away you want your puppy to be from you. City walking probably dictates a four footer while woods walking can be done on a much longer leash. Neighborhood walking is most comfortable on a six foot leash, perhaps with a handle part way up the length to allow you to rein in your pup as needed. Letting your pup run loose a bit in safe areas lends itself nicely to a thirty foot training lead that you can drop for freedom but step on if danger looms its ugly head. If you plan to step on a drag line of any sort, make sure it is attached to a harness and not a collar thus avoiding any tracheal pressure which is uncomfortable for your pup and potentially dangerous for his thyroid gland.

Whether or not to use a retractable leash is a bit of a tricky decision. Some reasons you might want to use this sort of leash are the freedom it allows thus providing more exercise than a short leash, the ability to travel further from you to go to the bathroom, and its retraction into the handle helping prevent legs from getting tangled up in the leash. Before you rush out to buy one, however, there are drawbacks to consider to using a retractable leash. First, the only way for a puppy to extend the retractable leash is to pull. Since most of us do not want our dogs to pull on the leash, using equipment that teaches the pup to pull may not appeal to you. Second, a retractable leash is easy to drop since it does not have a wrist loop as a soft leash does. If you do drop the base of the leash, it will start retracting on its own and sort of chase your puppy down the sidewalk, potentially scaring him, or, even worse, injuring him. Third, learning to use a retractable leash can be challenging. They have buttons to lock and unlock the mechanism and toggles to temporarily stop them from retracting. Like anything else, practice is needed to master all of this. Fourth, if you grab the nylon leash, instead of the handle, you can get quite a skin abrasion. Fifth, if you have long hair as I do, it can get tangled in the leash as it retracts creating quite a predicament. I will never forget the day this happened to me when I was walking two dogs at once, each on a retractable leash. I inadvertently bent over as one of the leashes retracted and my waist-length hair started to retract into the mechanism. In a panic, I yelled "STOP" to my dogs, a word they had never heard before. Since they had no idea what I was talking about, they did nothing and actually stopped to try to figure out this new language. This was a perfect reaction from the dogs, but purely good luck and not good thinking on my part. Anyway, I no longer use retractable leashes to walk my dogs. The cons outweigh the pros in my mind.

Managing Pulling

If you have a puppy that thinks pulling you down the sidewalk is some sort of canine moral obligation, you may want to use equipment that prevents or at least lessens the ability of the pup to pull. As with all equipment, there are many brands, prices and designs from which to choose. Harnesses that allow the leash to attach to the chest of the pup rather than the back are very effective. A few brands that come to mind are Easy Walk, SENSE-ible®

Several no-pull harnesses: SENSE-ible®, Easy Walk and Freedom.

and Sense-ation®. This design discourages pulling since when the pup attempts to drag you along, the front hooking location of the leash causes the dog to turn around facing you, which obviously stops the pulling. Other no-pull harnesses attach to the back but to an extra loop which tightens with pulling, again discouraging the practice. Other harnesses allow the leash to attach either on the chest or the back, depending on the situation. Some, such as the Freedom harness, also have a double ended leash available to attach to the front and the back simultaneously making it useful for powerful breeds. All of these harnesses come with instructions which should be read and followed. What you choose depends on how large your dog is and what sort of walker he is. In lieu of a harness, walking with the leash attached to a buckle collar and draped on the inside of one front leg keeps the attachment under the chin. This also helps manage pulling.

All of the devices above limit pulling by managing the behavior and not letting your pup practice what you don't want him to do. None, however, teach the dog how to walk on a loose lead, which is done as a separate activity. While you are teaching this, perhaps on a collar, use the harness to actually go for walks so you aren't undoing what you are teaching when you are trying to get your little beast some much needed exercise. If you want to fully train loose lead walking prior to hitting the streets, feel free to do so and exercise your pup in a different way letting him run or chase a ball in a fenced yard.

Teaching Loose Leash Walking

Walking a dog on a leash need not be water skiing on the sidewalk. Getting dragged hither and yon is unnecessary and makes walking drudgery instead of pleasurable. There are multiple ways to teach your pup not to pull, all of which work. You may prefer to use a combination of methods or pick one and stick with it.

The most common suggestion for stopping a pup from pulling on the leash is to stop when he pulls and walk when the leash is loose. The

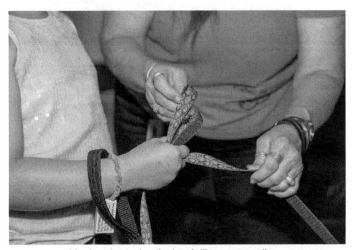

Maelyn shortening the leash like an accordian.

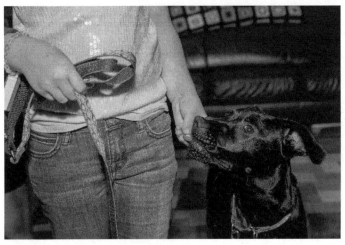

Maelyn holding the shortened leash in one hand with Sadie on her other side with the food lure.

reason this method works is because a dog will do whatever he can to get what he wants. If he wants to walk, he pulls to get you to walk and pulls harder to get you to walk faster. If the harder he pulls on the leash, the faster you walk, you are actually teaching him to pull since you are rewarding the pulling by walking faster. If you stop when he pulls, pulling becomes unsuccessful. When you stop, your pup may briefly pull harder to see if more effort is needed on his part. If you hold your ground, literally, he will do one of a few things. Your pup might turn around and look at you to see if you have gone into some sort of semi-coma. When he turns his head, the leash will become slightly loose and you can resume walking. Instead of looking back at you, your pup might choose to sit down when you stop walking. Again, this creates slack in the leash and you can move forward. A third response to your stopping is for your pup to continue to pull, hoping to eventually dislodge your shoulder's rotator cuff so the walk can resume. With this sort of persistent pulling, move from behind your pup to beside him but without lessening the tension he has created on the leash. Once you are next to him, the tense leash will cause him to sidestep slightly which creates a tiny amount of leash slack and you can then move forward. The biggest complaint I hear about the stop-and-go method described above is that it is beyond tedious since heavy pullers pull again as soon as forward motion is resumed. If your pup falls into this category, you may want to try something else.

Another common method to stop leash pulling is to turn around and walk the other way each time the pup pulls. This method can work, but if you have an actual destination, it becomes a bit frustrating to never reach it. I suggest this method only as a last resort or as an infrequently used option.

My favorite method for teaching loose leash walking is to use a clicker and cookies thus paying the pup to do what you want him to do. Don't get nervous: you won't have to walk the streets clicking and rewarding forever since the clicker is faded out of this activity after learning is achieved. To begin, decide which side you want your pup to walk on and load your pockets on that side with cookies. The most effective way I have found to hold a leash is to put the loop handle around your wrist and then pull the leash up between your index and middle fingers. If you have to shorten the length, accordion the leash in the palm of your hand and place the last section you folded between those two fingers. This method gives a firm grasp but is also releasable if you must let go. Lots of folks wrap the leash around their hand to control the length. This is unsafe since it heightens the chance of breaking your wrist if you need to let go of the leash and can't unwrap it fast enough.

For the training of loose lead walking, place the handle of the leash around the wrist on the opposite side of your body from your pup and place the clicker in the same hand before pulling the leash up between your fingers. In other words, if you want your pup on your left, put the leash handle around your right wrist and hold your clicker in your right hand, while putting cookies in your left side pocket. The leash can be draped either in front of your legs or behind your legs. Take one cookie in

your left hand and show it to your puppy who is next to your left leg. As you take a step forward, your pup will walk with you following the cookie. Continue to move forward a few steps, click while you are doing so, say "Walk" or "With Me", stop, feed the pup the cookie from your hand and, without moving forward, reload your left hand with another cookie. Repeat

Tom and Derek practicing getting Riley beside them, with a cookie lure.

the above, taking more steps each time before you click, stop and reward. Remember to always click WHILE you are walking and stop walking after you click to reward your pup. Most of us can't eat a hot fudge sundae on an escalator just as your pup probably can't enjoy his cookie if he has to keep walking while he eats. Click while walking, say "With Me", stop to feed, get another cookie in your hand, walk, "With Me", click, stop, feed, reload, etc. You may be thinking that this method is also pretty tedious, and you are correct, but it only lasts for a short while. Within one or two sessions, you can walk further and further between clicks. Soon, after stretching out the duration between rewards, you can stop having a cookie in your hand but only in your pocket. As you and your pup are moving forward, say "With me", click, stop, get out a cookie and feed, and move forward again. Before you know it, you will be able to walk around the block with only a few clicks and rewards.

Whatever method you use to teach your pup to walk properly, I suggest you plan each walk based on how much time you have, not how much distance you want to cover. Pups take a long time to go a short distance and if you are mileage oriented, your walk will be frustrating for you and your companion. Even walking older dogs should be time based. If you have thirty minutes, walk for fifteen and then head home. This time-based walking stops you from rushing your dog so you can, along with him, stop to smell the roses.

There are lots of opinions about where your pup should walk in relation to you. What I suggest is your pup should walk wherever it is convenient for you and fun for him. Walking next to you is sometimes a good choice, particularly when you are on a busy sidewalk, in an area where you want your pup close by instead of in the way of other pedestrians or in the face, more likely the butt, of other dogs. Walking next to you is accomplished pretty simply using the walking on a loose leash method described in detail in the section above.

What we haven't talked about, however, is what to do if your pup puts on the brakes and refuses to move when you want him walking next to you. If your pup does this often, you may want to consider what is causing the behavior. If he stops short and doesn't want to move toward the end of your walk, you may be going too far and he is simply tired. If you suspect this, let him rest before finishing the walk and don't walk as far your next time out. If your pup does this in the same place every walk, it may be that something in that area frightened your pup, perhaps even something you didn't notice.

Candy luring Maggie to move along during a walk.

There may be a predator's scent on the sidewalk, a dog barking inside a nearby house, a loud truck passing by in this area yesterday, or a zillion other options. In this situation, try using a cookie lure to get him walking next to you again and once you are past the scary place, he should be fine. Pups also sometimes put on

Heather with Ajax and Candy with Maggie out for a relaxed walk.
Photo by Rae O'Leary

123

the brakes as soon as you leave your own property. This is simply concern about leaving the nest, so to speak. You can try luring with a cookie, but if this doesn't work, don't force the issue. Turning a walk into a power struggle is not the way to go. If you really want to leash walk but your pup won't leave the yard on a leash, take him for a short ride in the car, park and walk him home. You can retrieve your car later. By using one or more of these approaches, your pup can be taught to walk nicely at your side. Should you always expect this to be the way you walk together? Probably not.

'Go Sniff'

Dogs love to sniff. They sniff everything. They sniff us, they sniff each other, they sniff the air, they sniff the ground. Dogs sniff. They "see" with their noses. They can sniff out cancer, smoke, illegal drugs, missing people, seizure activity, endangered wildlife and bedbugs. Dogs sniff. Instead of trying to stop the sniffing, why not embrace it, at

Candy and Heather keeping their dogs next to them when meeting. Photo by Rae O'Leary

least some of the time. One way to embrace this sniffing is to encourage your puppy to sniff his way along for a portion of your leash walks. All you have to do is release the 'With Me' cue, lengthen the amount of leash he has and he will do the rest. When he begins to sniff, which he will, tell him "Go Sniff". Once you connect this cue to what he is doing, you can use it as a release from 'With Me'. If your pup wants to move along as he sniffs, let him do so. Go with him. Enjoy watching him doing what he is best at: smelling stuff you can't smell. The nose of a dog is an amazing organ. Sniff walks are a great way to spend time together in the woods or on the sidewalk. Whenever you need to move along, simply cue him "With Me" and off you go.

If your pup is the sort who may try to chase wildlife when in sniff-mode, keep the elbow of your leash arm bent and locked, for two reasons. If he does try to take off, a bent, locked elbow is more effective at preventing his sucess (the bunny will thank you). Additionally, you are less apt to suffer a shoulder injury if your pup suddenly jerks forward and catches you off guard.

Walk Behind Me

Just as you can teach your pup to walk next to you or to sniff out his own path in front of you, you can also teach him to walk behind you. Why would you want to do this? Walking behind you can come in very handy in many situations. Some pups can be nervous about people or dogs walking toward them. If you teach your pup to go behind you when others approach, he feels safer. Then, when he shows you he wants to go forward, you can let him.

Candy teaching Maggie 'Behind'.

Some pups are obsessed with wildlife such as squirrels or chipmunks. They just can't function in the presence of these creatures. This situation can be managed just as you handled the fear of approaching strangers. Ask your dog to stay behind you

Heather keeping Ajax behind her as Candy and Maggie pass by. Photo by Rae O'Leary

either until he calms down or until the creature moves on. I once owned a dog who broke a leather leash trying to chase a squirrel. It couldn't be allowed to happen again since he took off and couldn't even hear me calling him. That's squirrel addiction. I did get him back fairly quickly and safely but that was more luck than anything else. I didn't want a repeat of that... ever. I took him home and in the house, on a leash, I lured him behind me with a cookie, clicked, said "Behind", rewarded with the cookie and released with "Done". I repeated this until I could cue him to go behind me by saying "Behind". Finally, I taught him to stay behind me as we walked, until I released him. He never broke another leash. As soon as either of us saw a squirrel in our path, I would say "Behind" and he would, although begrudgingly, get behind me and stay there until further notice. That was one of the best things I taught that dog. It probably saved his life and most certainly saved my shoulder!

All in all, there is a lot involved in walking your pup on leash. You only have to teach the areas of leash walking that are helpful to you and/or your pup. Pick and choose, knowing you can always teach additional leash behaviors if you need to. The bottom line: walking your pup should be fun for you and fun for your pup. If it isn't, investigate what needs to change and cause it to happen. You and your clicker will be able to do it.

Chapter 13

Four on the Floor

Rob teaching Sadie 'Off' to prevent jumping.

"Oh, it's okay. I don't mind." That is the biggest fib ever and it is frequently the response you get from neighbors and visitors when your puppy jumps on them. You know what? It's not okay for your pup to jump on your neighbors, guests, or you and put their possibly muddy paws all over humans. Your puppy is just doing what feels good to him so let's show him another way. Teaching your little pogo sticking puppy to properly greet pedestrians on the sidewalk or visitors in your home is well worth the little bit of effort required to do so.

Jumping on People

Jumping on people takes many forms. Some puppies jump on family members, some jump on only certain family members, some jump on only visitors, some jump on only some visitors, some jump on passersby on the sidewalk, and, you guessed it, some jump on only some passersby on the sidewalk. So here's the good news: all of the above can be fixed with the same techniques and there are a few from which to choose.

First and foremost, as we have discussed in other chapters, don't give your puppy the opportunity to practice a behavior you or others don't like. When it comes to jumping on people, prevention goes a long way and it comes in the form of a leash. Once you identify the people who are your pet's potential victims, be ready prior to the jumping taking place. It is perfectly acceptable for your little creature to be in your presence dragging a leash. Unsupervised, this can be hazardous since the leash can get stuck or, worse yet, tangled on furniture causing it to topple onto your pup. But if you are right there with your pup, leash dragging can be quite effective in preventing jumping since you can pretty quickly put a foot on the leash when his energy level starts to escalate. Using a foot rather than picking up the leash with your hand is preferable since your hand is connected by your forearm to your elbow. When you hold a leash in your hand and your puppy pulls to leap on a guest, your elbow will give a bit, inadvertently telling your pup that if he just tugs a bit harder he might be successful. On the other hand, or rather foot, if you step on the leash and the pup jumps, he gets nowhere. All you have to do to prevent successful jumping is place the ball of your foot on the leash giving him one inch less leash than length of leg. Keep slack in the leash between your foot and the pup so he doesn't feel pinned, but, if he goes to jump up, he won't have enough length of leash to do so. Get it? This really works and it works immediately when it comes to preventing jumping. Prevention, however, is not enough. It is important to teach your pup not to pogo his way through life.

One very effective way to teach a pup not to jump is the human anchor method. To accomplish this, one human holds the handle of the pup's leash with two hands and then anchors his hands and elbows close to his body. Presto, there you have it, a human anchor. The second human does the approach, beginning several yards away from the pup who is tethered to the human anchor. No one talks during this exercise, not to each other and not to the puppy. A lot of communication takes place, but none of it is verbal. So, picture this: a puppy is connected to a human by

Candy as a human anchor for Maggie.

The approach is completed once Maggie is calm.

a leash, the puppy sees the second human approaching and goes to the end of the leash, probably on two hind legs, trying desperately to get to the person to jump on him. In response, the approaching human turns his back on the pup, saying nothing, and waits. As soon as the puppy calms, the approaching human turns to face the pup and slowly takes a step toward him. If the pup remains calm, the human takes a second step. If the pup begins to pull on the leash, the approaching person turns away from the pup again, waiting for calm behavior. It may take up to five minutes to actually get to the pup the first time you try this. But, since we are allowing the puppy to learn this on his own with trial and error, once he gets it, he really gets it. I have had puppies stay calm in as few as two attempts, much to the owners' surprise. Ironically, the more the puppy is desperate for you to get to him, the quicker he figures out how to "make" you keep coming to him: by staying calm.

Since it is not always convenient to have your puppy on a leash or to spend five minutes letting your puppy figure out you want him to be calm before you will approach him, another method to supplement the above is a good idea. This method involves teaching the pup a verbal cue which instructs him to keep his feet on the floor. As always, any word will do but consistent use of the same word is important. The most commonly used cue is 'Off', telling your puppy to keep his feet 'Off' of the guests. The technique employed here is called spatial pressure, meaning that you push a tsunami of air toward your puppy without actually touching him. When your puppy is approaching you, hold both of your hands together in front of you with your arms outstretched forming a sort of shield, and rock with one foot in front of the other toward the puppy, saying the word "Off". When your puppy reaches you, switch your hands to a palm up position, hook a thumb in the collar to prevent nose bopping and use your free fingers to affectionately scritch your puppy's

Candy employing the use of a kettlebell as an anchor to practice 'Off' alone with Maggie.

Rewarding Maggie for being calm.

neck as you praise him for keeping his feet on the floor. As you begin to stand up, your pup might then think it is okay to jump on you, so quickly repeat the 'Off' rocking shield maneuver to ensure continued success. If you happen to be unlucky enough to have a relentlessly jumping puppy and young children who can't be consistent with this body language, arm them with actual toy shields or the lids from large plastic storage bins to place between themselves and the puppy. This is a quick fix to a difficult situation.

If jumping on arriving guests is the issue, make sure your puppy is on a leash prior to opening the door. This is hard to accomplish if you are running around like a nut trying to find a leash while your door bell is repeatedly ringing. To avoid this pitfall, simply have an extra leash that is always kept by the door. You can answer the doorbell ringing with "Just a minute", and leash your pup prior to opening the door. As your guest

enters, keep your pup at your side by clicking and rewarding him to stay next to you. Create a cue for greeting such as 'Go Greet' or 'Say Hi' and then let your pup go forward toward the guest. Before he arrives, step between your puppy and your visitor and do your 'Off' technique. If your guest likes dogs, he can praise and pet your pup as you remind him to remain 'Off'.

The leash handle can be attached to the inside doorknob, closing the door on the leash to create an anchor.

There are some puppies who get really wild when they know someone is at the door. Knocking and bell ringing just drives this type of puppy nuts with excite-ment! If you are unlucky enough to have this version of guest jump-

Candy praising Maggie for being calm while anchored to the doorknob.

131

ing, more than what is described above is warranted. This pup needs to be kept behind you, completely behind you, as described in Chapter 12. Once he is calm in the 'Behind' position, you can then give a 'Go Greet' or 'Say Hi' cue and go into 'Off' mode. Practicing for this sort of pup is a must, as preparation for what is needed when actual guests show up on the doorstep. Practice each time a family member gets home by having them ring the doorbell prior to entering. Another family member who is already home can act as if this is a guest arriving thus creating a teachable moment. An active household can get in a lot of practice using the daily comings and goings of members as opportunities to work on 'Behind' and 'Off'. When at least two family members are home, you can also practice by having one person leave the house by the back door, come to the front door and ring the doorbell. The more teachable moments you can create, the quicker your pup will habituate to doorbell ringing and staying calm when greeting visitors.

Jumping on Furniture

Whether or not you want your puppy on your furniture is your choice. There are as many reasons to allow our pets on our beds, chairs and couches as there are reasons not to do so. Can't decide? Members of your family disagree? The best rule of thumb in this case is to begin with a no furniture rule and loosen up if you decide to do so. Once a pup is used to getting up on your sofa, either alone or with members of your family, the decision is made: he's allowed on the furniture.

Believe it or not, this is not an all or nothing proposition. Your little furry beast is smart enough to be taught he's welcome on some pieces of furniture but not others. Yup, it's true. Another surprising fact is you can teach your pup he is only allowed up with an invitation from you or another family member. The default is to stay 'Off' unless invited. He can also learn he is allowed on furniture when it is covered with a throw, sheet or blanket but not when the covering is removed. Remember the "dogs lead blind people through intersections" statement? They are smart with a capital S. That being said, before you can teach your pup what you want, you have to know what you want and be consistent about it. It is not wise to have some family members sneaking the pup up for a snuggle when the house rule is not to do so. This will really confuse your puppy with mixed messages, particularly if the same people have different rules at different times. So, on with it.

If you want your pup on any furniture he chooses, that's pretty easy to accomplish. Simply pat the cushion as you say "Up" and you're done. If you want your pup on some furniture but not on other furniture, approach those he is allowed on and tell him "Up". When you approach the forbidden surfaces, go into 'Off' mode by using your hands as a shield and rocking toward your puppy with the spatial pressure technique we used to prevent jumping on people. The key here, however, is consistency. The pup should NEVER be allowed to get on the forbidden furniture, even when you're busy, even when you're tired and even when you're not home. That forbidden furniture must be inaccessible to the puppy at all times. If all the furniture in an entire room is off limits, simply close the door to that room or put a baby gate in the doorway so the pup is only in that room when you are supervising and training. If only some furniture in a room is forbidden fruit and you want the puppy to have access to the other furniture in the room, simply put empty laundry baskets, big cardboard boxes or unused baby gates on the surface of the forbidden furniture. Be creative: there are about a gazillion ways to protect a chair or couch from your little beast. If you don't want your dog on furniture unless it is covered with a sheet, blanket or throw, that is pretty simple. Put the covering on, tell him "Up" and then remove the pup and the covering and tell him "Off". When you aren't teaching, simply keep the covering on so the pup isn't in trouble for breaking house rules when he helps himself to a comfortable, blanketed chair. As you can see, you have a lot of choices here. You really can teach your pup anything you want to teach him, as long as you are patient and consistent. Really.

Getting in the Dishwasher

Many folks feel that the dishwasher's rinse cycle should be performed by the dishwasher, not their puppy. If you agree, teach your pup to stay away from this appliance when you open the door to unload clean dishes, or, worse yet, load in food laden dishes after a meal. Believe it or not, this lesson can frequently be taught in a single session or a few at most. Start when your dishwasher contains a load that has already been cleaned. As you begin to open the door to the machine, tell your pup "Off" and go into your rocking shield stance. If he approaches, close the dishwasher door and begin again. You can also use the action of opening the dishwasher door as an 'Off' cue. Close the door if the puppy continues to approach. Repeat until your puppy gets the message and praise as he stays back from the opening door. After your next meal, repeat all of the above when you are loading the dirty plates into the dishwasher. Take your time, closing the door as often as needed to be clear to your puppy that he is not to approach. Soon your pup will find the dishwasher loading and unloading to be pretty boring and he will entertain himself elsewhere when you are busy cleaning up after a meal.

You may be wondering why a clicker and cookies are not involved here. My reasoning is to make the entire meal cleanup boring for your puppy. If you click and reward this activity, your puppy may continue to bother you around the dishwasher in order to stay 'Off' in order to get clicked. In this particular case, boring is better. We are simply saying, "Nothing here for you, little one."

Teaching your pup to stay 'Off' of furniture, people and appliances can go a long way to creating a well behaved pup who is a pleasure to have around. Don't forget, however, when you bring your pup to someone else's home, find out their rules in advance and help your puppy to comply. It would be sad for him to be seen as troublesome, when he's just being a puppy. Keep your pup leashed if need be, particularly if you allow your pup on your furniture but your mother-in-law does not. Your puppy is exactly that, your puppy. Help him to follow new rules in new locations and everyone is happy.

Teaching Kendall 'Off' by rocking toward her.

Giving Kendall affection for staying on the floor.

Lorin teaching Kendall 'Off'.

Chapter 14

Bait and Switch:
Dealing with Stealing and Destruction

Nikita and Finnick have destroyed a dog bed.   Finnick trying to sleep on what is left of the bed.
Photos by owner.

Some of the most annoying puppy habits include stealing house-hold items, refusing to let go of items we want them to relinquish and destroying items that belong to us or to them. Why do puppies do these things? The cause may seem to be premeditated revenge or defiance but, in reality, puppies are only being puppies and playing with whatever is in their path. They repeat behaviors that are, in their eyes, success-ful. What is successful? For puppies, success can be behaviors that are just plain fun to do. Success can be behaviors that get them cookies or attention. Success can be behaviors that get them physical touch from their humans. Stealing and destroying ALWAYS get lots of attention from the human members of the household and can even start a really fun game of chase. Holding onto items desired by the humans also gets attention and even physical touch as attempts are made to pry open the pups' mouths, often without success. Destroying stuff can be fun, making lots of funny tearing and crunching noises. Unfortunately, the very behaviors humans find the most annoying and, even dangerous, can be a bit tricky to stop without inadvertently making those same behaviors get the pups what they want: attention, physical touch and play. Let's explore how to be successful in stopping such behaviors, while encouraging play that works for both of you.

'Trade' for Stolen Items

Cell phones, remote controls, shoes, underwear or things you mistakenly drop on the floor are considered fair game to many puppies. Most of these items have a delicious human aroma which attracts puppies. The reaction they get from their humans is a huge benefit since most people will stop whatever they are doing and chase down a pup to retrieve a cell phone or favorite running shoe. Chasing, however, is the absolutely worst thing you can do when your puppy runs away from you with a valuable item. First, a game of chase is a huge reward to a puppy. NEVER chase a puppy, even in play. When I work with families with young children, I explain that chasing a puppy around the yard teaches your puppy one thing and one thing only: humans cannot catch puppies! That is one of the last things you want your puppy to know. Second, a puppy loves the game of chase. It's fun. If stealing causes a chase and a chase is fun, your puppy will continue to steal to start another game of chase. Third, a puppy is much more likely to swallow an item he is holding in his mouth if he is chased. Remember we talked about dogs being scavengers? What better way for a scavenger to protect what he has stolen than to swallow it?

If it's a bad idea to chase your puppy to get back your flip-flop, what are you supposed to do? I suggest you play 'Trade'. When you see your puppy grab something he shouldn't, instead of running after him, run the other way toward the toy box or the cookie jar. Get a squeaky toy or some cookies your puppy loves that preferably have a noisy wrapper or are in a shakable container that rattles. When your puppy hears the squeaky toy or the rattling of the cookie jar, he will come running back, with or without the item he stole. When you see him drop the item, whether it is a distance from you or when he arrives at your side, say the word "Trade" which puts a word on the action of dropping the item. Next, 'Trade' the item for a toy or a cookie. What you do after that is the most important piece of the learning process. If your pup dropped the item a distance from you, interest him in a toy or another cookie in your hand as you approach the dropped, stolen item. Pick the item up off the floor, put it in front of your puppy and say "Leave It" (see Chapter 6). If he tries to get it, protect the item so he can't grab it and repeat the 'Leave It' cue until your puppy seems resigned to the fact he can't have it back. Then simply remove the item and put it away. Do NOT reward your puppy for the 'Leave It' portion of this process. You used a toy or cookie to get your puppy to come to you without chasing him, but do not use a reward after you remind him that he shouldn't have taken it to begin with. It is this second part of the process that will reduce the pup's desire to steal. Who wants a cookie-free lesson of 'Leave It'? No one. If your puppy is stealing stuff before you have taught him 'Leave It', do 'Trade' none the less, but skip the 'Leave It' section. Not rewarding by chasing overrides using food to get the item back, although teaching 'Leave It' in the near future is needed to truly reduce your pup's thievery.

What 'Trade' ends up teaching your puppy is that he isn't to run away with your belongings and he needs to give them back to you if he succumbs to the temptation to take something in the first place. As time goes on, if he grabs something he shouldn't, when you tell him to 'Trade', he will just stand still and drop the item as you approach. You will no longer need to use a toy or cookie but simply the verbal cue to 'Trade'.

Playing 'Tug' / Ending 'Tug'

In addition 'Trade', it is also very useful to teach your puppy to allow items he has in his mouth to be taken from him, whether it is his own toy or something he has stolen. This differs from 'Trade' which means to stop running and drop the item. We will teach a cue such as 'Give' or 'Out' to allow you to take the item from his mouth as he opens it. Prying a puppy's mouth open is difficult, dangerous and unnecessary once 'Give' is learned.

The fastest way to teach 'Give' is when the puppy has a toy and wants you to tug on it. Most pups love to play 'Tug', and, as long as he has learned 'Leave It' and 'Give', tug is a very rewarding and beneficial game to play. There is a lot of information available telling you NOT to play 'Tug' with your pup. Many people claim this game will cause aggression and turn your pup into a biter. This is not the case when 'Tug'

is played properly. So, you ask, how do you play 'Tug' properly? First of all, 'Tug' should be played with a toy you have in YOUR toy box, not in the pup's. The tug toy starts and ends in your hands. When you first present the toy, tell your puppy to 'Leave It' and keep the toy in your

Sadie biting too close to Ryan's hand which results in a 'Give' cue.

possession but in the full view of your puppy. If he goes to grab it, protect it as you protected the cookies on the floor when you first taught him 'Leave It'. Once he can look at the tug toy without grabbing it, make it wiggle and tell him 'Tug'. As he grabs it, provide slight resistance (baby teeth can be a bit delicate) to make the game fun for your puppy. This game of 'Tug' actually simulates the predatory sequence which is natural to meat

Maelyn playing tug with Sadie.

eaters who used to have to hunt down and catch their meals. Although domestic dogs don't need to do that to survive, they still enjoy the process immensely. When you want to end the 'Tug' portion of the game, keep your hands on the toy but let it go limp in the pup's mouth. To cause him to open his mouth, move your hands toward his muzzle, one on each side and apply very slight inward pressure. As the puppy begins to open his mouth, roll the toy down and out of his released grip, saying "Give" as he does so. Then, immediately go into 'Leave it' mode with the toy right in front of the pup but protected by your hands as much as necessary. Wiggle the toy, say "Tug" again, allow him to grab it, play the game and repeat "Give". What we have taught "Give" to actually mean is "open your mouth". The 'Give' word can then be used to ask the pup to release and put into your hand whatever he has in his mouth, preventing the destruction of the item or, worse yet, injury to your puppy.

There are some puppies who do not open their mouths when slight inward pressure is applied. For those pups, use a cookie to cause the mouth to open, saying "Give" as the mouth opens to drop the tug toy and take the cookie.

Prevent, Prevent, Prevent

Teaching takes time, as you know. While you are teaching your puppy 'Leave It' (Chapter 6), 'Trade' and 'Give', it is really crucial to prevent stealing and destruction. Failure to do so can result in quite a mess in your home, can cause your puppy to ingest dangerous items such as batteries, sharp objects, strings that can ball up in the intestine or many other undesirable episodes. Prevention comes in many forms: doors that can be shut, baby gates in doorways, X-pens, tethers and crates. If your human child has a messy room with toys everywhere, keep the puppy out of that room. If you have a huge toxic plant in the corner of your living room, put an X-pen around it. X-pens are designed to be used as a bottomless playpen for puppies but I seldom put a puppy in one. It's possible to put everything BUT the puppy in X-pens, both indoors and out: woodstoves, Christmas trees, coffee tables laden with food for guests, outdoor Rhododendrons, and anything else needing puppy protection. I have even been known to put a whole family in an X-pen to keep my pups away from those afraid of dogs during a party.

Puppies just want to have fun and unrolling the entire roll of toilet paper qualifies. Guess who needs to keep that bathroom door shut? Puppies learn to jump up on chairs left pulled out from a table to gain access to leftover food. Guess who needs to push in the chairs and/or put the leftovers away? Puppies love to swallow socks and underwear. Guess who needs to put socks and underwear in the washer, the dryer, the hamper, the drawer or on their feet? You've got it! All of this prevention is temporary, just until your puppy is taught how to follow house rules. Teaching takes time, management is instant.

Chapter 15

I Heard You the First Time: Barking Issues

Mensa barking.

People talk, dogs bark, puppies learn to bark. Your pup may or may not have found his voice yet, but it is a good idea to be prepared in case he becomes too talkative. Be cautious here, however, since puppies express themselves through barking. There is a fine line between communication barking and nuisance barking: one is desirable, one is not. Let's begin to determine the difference and to limit the barking you and your pup can live without.

LOOK AT ME: Barking for Attention

Your puppy uses barking to let you know he needs you. When a puppy needs to pee and he is crated, he whines or barks to ask to be brought outside to relieve himself. Once a puppy has learned not to use the human house as a bathroom, he whines or barks at the door to let you know he needs your help with the doorknob since he doesn't have thumbs. When you respond to this barking, as you should, you are also teaching your pup that his voice can be used to get what he needs and he will make use of that newfound skill as he sees fit. Some of his choices of when to use his voice may not be desirable. Barking wildly at you so you will give him attention or a cookie falls within this category. One day I was meeting with a new client whose dog, when bored, would bark at her kitchen cupboard. She would excuse herself from our conversation, open the cupboard and give him a cookie. This happened several times within a half hour span. My client was so intent on stopping the interruption, she didn't realize she was rewarding her dog. He, however, figured it out immediately and was having a blast. Smart dog and a great example of a dog being opportunistic!

It's important to pay attention to what you pay your pup to do. Rewarding inappropriate demands is viewed as encouragement by the puppy. Simultaneously, there is a shift in the relationship from one of teacher/student to one that resembles permissive parent/naughty child. Kind, consistent teaching and gentle consequences are where we want to go with our canine companions. Very simply stated, pay what you like and ignore, manage or provide pain/fear free results for what you don't like. This universal simplicity applies to barking. When your puppy barks, always check out the cause. Does he need to go to the bathroom? Is his water bowl empty? Is it dinner time and you're engrossed in texting a friend? Is his tail on fire? None of the above? Maybe he is bored and you are his source of entertainment. This is fine, to a degree, but pups are able to be taught to self-entertain. If he is loudly demanding you play with him, don't. If he is demanding a cookie for no other reason than he wants one, don't give him one. If he is screaming at you to pet him, resist.

So what should you do? How do you accomplish not giving into demands and, more importantly, teach your pup to ask for something politely? Your response to loud attention-seeking barking is to turn your back on the pup. If the barking escalates, which it most likely will, take a step further away, still not looking at your pup. This shunning is done silently since even talking to a demanding pup will reinforce the noise by providing attention when you don't want to do so. As soon as your puppy is silent, even for an instant, turn and give him the attention he wants. Redirect his bored brain to a brief teaching session by working on any of the behaviors he is learning. If the barking resumes, turn away, silently, once again. As soon as silence occurs, give attention. A word of caution here: it is important to build the duration of the silence quickly since, otherwise, all you are teaching is bark, stop barking, get what you want, bark, stop barking, get what you want. Since this isn't what YOU want, you need to move toward your pup staying silent to get the attention he wants. Your goal is to have a dog who communicates politely, not in a demanding "right now" sort of way. To build this duration, simply don't turn back toward the pup until he can stay silent for more than an instant. If he barks again while you are waiting, stay turned away until he understands you are waiting for a brief extension of the quiet behavior before you turn toward him. Most pups get this pretty quickly, and yours will too.

Teaching the Word 'Quiet'

In addition to turning away from a noisy, demanding pup, it is wise to teach him a word to let him know when you want his barking to cease. As always, use a word that you can remember and make sure all of your family members are using the same word.

Common choices are 'Quiet', 'Enough', 'Stop' or whatever else you can think of as long as you teach it to your pup. The most effective way to teach this new vocabulary is a method called capturing. You capture quiet moments and attach a label to them. Bear with me for a moment, for what I am about to tell you won't make sense when you first read it. All you are going to do is click when your pup is quiet, say "Quiet" (or whatever word you've chosen) and give him a cookie. Repeat and end the session. A bit later, do this again: click, say "Quiet", repeat once or twice and walk away. Your pup will have absolutely no idea what you are clicking but he won't refuse what he considers to be a free cookie. After you have been capturing these silent moments for a few days, the real teaching begins. The next time your pup nuisance barks, shun him while you wait for a brief, silent moment. When it occurs, click, say "Quiet" and reward. Your pup will recognize the word you have been teaching him when he is naturally silent and it all comes together in the creation of a cue to ask him to stop barking. As we did earlier to stop attention barking, quickly begin to build duration to avoid inadvertently teaching your pup to bark in order to elicit "Quiet" with a cookie reward. Do this by responding to the bark with the cue "Quiet" but don't click the instant he complies; have him STAY quiet, briefly at first, prior to clicking. Continue to extend the duration of 'Quiet' over the next few days. You want your pup to stop barking and to remain silent once the cue is given. Once taught, you can use this cue for barking no matter what is causing your puppy to explode into a noisy ball of fur.

DON'T LEAVE ME: Separation Barking

Your puppy likes to be with you. Companionship is one of the biggest benefits of having a pet so we choose a pet that likes to be near us: a dog. There are times, however, that companionship takes on a whole new meaning when your pup won't allow you to be out of his sight without throwing a canine fit! When this issue gets out of hand it is referred to as separation anxiety which can be a serious problem. Since you have a young pup, you can do a lot to prevent separation issues from developing.

Having your pup with you a good deal of the time is a good thing. Having your pup never, ever out of your sight is not a good thing. Right from the beginning, crate your pup and leave the room briefly. Return, let him out of the crate and go about your day. Do this frequently, varying the duration, so your pup learns being away from you is a normal part of life. If your pup complains when you leave, NEVER come back into sight while whining or barking is occurring. Obviously I am not referring to a pup who has been asleep in his crate and wakes up telling you he needs to go outside to relieve himself. This is not a separation issue but a very important part of house training. The reference here is when a pup is crated to keep him safe while you leave the room. If your pup instantly says, "No way am I staying here alone!", he needs to learn he is safe and able to be comfortable when you crate him. Leaving him often and briefly will make the necessary absences less of an issue.

What do you do if your pup is a complainer right from the start? You can teach him being quiet will cause you to return. Gradually, build duration. When your pup has recently been outside for a bathroom trip so you know he doesn't need to relieve himself, bring him to his crate. Give him a cookie for going in (or lure him in using a cookie if he hasn't yet learned to go in on his own), secure the crate door and disappear. Don't respond to his whining or barking but be ready to click as soon as the noise pauses, even if it is only an inhale. Right after you click, you say "Quiet" and return to give your pup a reward. Repeat a few times and end the session. If, at any point in this routine, he doesn't immediately start whining as you latch the crate, click, say "Quiet", reward and repeat prior

148

to any whining or barking. As you build duration, there will be times the barking starts up again before you click. When this happens, you have to wait until he pauses so you can click and return to give a cookie. One of the many benefits of using a clicker is you can mark 'Quiet' when you are out of the pup's sight. Once you click, the pup will most likely remain silent waiting for you to appear and give him a cookie. This pregnant pause between the click and the cookie is magical in helping you build duration, so use it to your benefit.

Think back to Chapter 8 when we discussed 'Wait' and having a phrase for your pup waiting at the door when you are leaving without him. 'I'll be back' is the phrase that fit the bill, and it can also be used when dealing with separation barking. When you crate your pup preparing to go out of sight, tell him "I'll be back" and leave. Click when he is silent, say "Quiet" and return to reward. Using a known phrase, prior to disappearing, gives your pup information about what you are about to do and can help him feel more comfortable with your brief disappearing act. Making your exit a practiced routine will hold you in good stead when you have to leave for longer periods such as going to work, shopping or out to dinner. A pup cannot be left longer than a few hours until he is physically mature enough to be without bathroom access. Any required duration should be built slowly ensuring the pup's needs are accommodated. Learning to sleep quietly in his crate until your return is a skill your pup should, and will, have if you teach him from the beginning this will be a part of his life. A word of caution: if, during your absence, your pup is violently destructive, drools excessively, soils his crate or tries to escape, he may be struggling with separation anxiety. Please consult a canine behavior professional for assistance.

LOOK OUT!!!!!!: Alarm Barking

In addition to barking for attention and barking when left alone, pups also bark when an unexpected noise, object or even a scent enters the scene. This type of barking is referred to as alarm barking and should be handled very differently from the other types. Alarm barking can be very useful to us, since its cause may be something we, as humans, are not aware of but perhaps should be. Targets for alarm barking include people walking by your house or car, ringing doorbells, dogs or wildlife entering your yard (even after dark), trash cans appearing on the sidewalk on collection day, sirens whirring in the distance, sudden and unexpected noises, or even shadows on the wall. My favorite saying for alarm bark-

Glitter barking at a stranger on the porch. "Thank you", Glitter.

ing is "Always trust the dog." If your dog says there is something there, he's right. Granted, it could be as benign as a chipmunk sitting on a log, but there is always a cause for alarm barking. Since we don't know the cause until we investigate, NEVER extinguish this sort of barking: limit it, yes; extinguish it, no.

I will never forget when a client called me to his home to help with alarm barking. As I proceeded to tell him we didn't want his dog to stop doing this altogether but only stop when told, a look of relief washed over his face. He told me his neighbor had hired a trainer to stop his dog from barking and the trainer had done just that: stopped all barking. A few weeks later, said neighbor was in the shower and, as his dog sat silently watching, his home was stripped of all his electronics by a burglar. I can see the thought bubble over his dog's head: "You don't want me to bark? Even now?"

How do you limit barking? Teaching the cue 'Quiet' is the beginning, which you have already learned to do. Now, however, you want to add a few steps. Since you want to reinforce the initial alert, do so by acknowledging the bark verbally by saying "What's up?" and visually by checking the direction your pup is barking. At first, actually go to the window or door where he is barking (later you can do this without getting up). Then confirm that he does, in fact, have cause, even if you don't know what it is and that you will handle it. Confirmation can take any form you want with some choices being "We're safe", "I've got it", "Enough", or even "Quiet". Once you have acknowledged and confirmed, it is time to redirect the pup away from the cause. You can do this by removing the pup from the window and bringing him to the kitchen for some 'Leave It' (Chapter 6) practice. Another great redirection is to play 'Find It' (Chapter 6) for a few minutes, until he forgets what he was barking at. You can also redirect by removing access such as closing a door or pulling a shade. If the source of the barking is an object that is unfamiliar to the pup, you may want to use a different technique, allowing the pup to approach and touch the object if it is safe to do so. Never force an approach as this could elicit fear or increase existing fear. You approach the object, modeling it is safe to do so and click/reward each forward-moving step of the pup. If he can't continue to approach, wait until he appears to be calm and then you can end the session.

Outside Barking

Alarm barking when your pup is outside in a fenced yard is very similar to other alarm barking and also should be limited. If your pup sends a squirrel up a tree and barks at it sitting there on an out-of-reach branch, tell him "Quiet". If he continues, bring him inside. Wait briefly and let him outside again. If the barking resumes, say "Quiet" and if he doesn't respond, bring him in. Repeat this procedure until he learns that to be able to stay outside, he needs to be quiet when told. A common mistake is to bring the barking pup in for the rest of the day. The lesson will be lost, since it is the repetitive cause and effect that creates the teachable moment. My own dogs have a doggy door, actually two doggy doors. They were taught as puppies when they were outside and I was inside, a knock on the window would cause a flurry of cookies to appear on the floor as they came through the doggy door. I then sent them right back out to continue playing and exploring. I would repeat this knocking jack-pot of cookies often enough that they couldn't resist a window knock even when they were barking at a chipmunk or other invader. Once my husband watched me do this, he learned to do it, too. His twist on it, however, was less successful: every time he knocked and they came in, he shut the doggy door so he could go back to what he was doing. I explained to him that this would soon backfire on him and they would stop coming in for the knock since they would associate it with the end of outdoor time. We always need to be careful to really think things through from the perspective of the pup. Oh, another word of caution: when you go out to bring your pup in, don't chase him around the yard, thus rewarding unwanted behavior. You may be able

Karen's dog Morgan barking as only a Corgi can.
Photo by Stuart Tucker

to tell him "Sit", "Stay" and then retrieve him. If that doesn't work, he may have to go out dragging a long line. When you go out to get him, put a foot somewhere on the twenty or so feet of rope and walk on the rope until you get to the pup. Leash him and bring him in.

Nuisance barking of any type can be difficult to limit. Some pups bark more than others and some can be very noisy indeed. Once all of the above techniques are employed, additional measures may still be needed to, literally, keep your happy home and to keep your home happy. Barking for a minute or two at a treed squirrel may be okay at two in the afternoon, but not at five in the morning. Barking at knocking on your door may be fine but, if you live in an apartment building, barking every, single time someone has the nerve to walk down the shared hallway may not be so fine. If you must stop barking at a certain time of day or in a specific situation that has zero tolerance, you may have to go to a humane form of control. Don't panic; there is never a need to hurt or scare your pup with electric shock or a squirt of citronella in the muzzle area. It may be necessary, however, to annoy your pup so that his annoying barking stops. The annoyance is available in either auditory or tactile form. The auditory version is ultrasonic sound that occurs with repeated barking. There are sound collars the dog wears or boxes that can be placed in your home or yard. Let me caution you, the ultrasonic method should only be employed in single dog households since all other dogs present, barking or not, will be subject to the annoying sound waves caused when one dog barks. Another type of control is the vibration collar that is NOT equipped to deliver electric shock. The collar has a small plastic box that sits over the larynx. When the pup barks, it causes the box to vibrate much the way a cell phone or pager vibrates. There are a few pups that may be frightened by the vibration and its use should be discontinued. Most just find it annoying enough to stop barking but not so annoying as to be upset by it. There can be no other collar on the pup when he is wearing the vibration collar since the friction between the two collars will cause it to activate. Only use the collar when absolutely necessary or the pup may adjust to the vibration and it will cease to be annoying. You want it to work when needed, so don't overdo it.

Barking is normal and natural for pups. Incessant barking, however, is a problem for neighbors, other dogs and your family. Proper teaching and management will allow your pup to bark as needed but put a damper on nuisance barking that is unnecessary for both your pup and everyone else. Whoops, gotta go. My neighbor just got home from work and my dogs are barking at the slamming of the car door. Can't let that continue...

Conclusion

Puppies are a lot of fun. They are cute and cuddly and funny. It is hard to be in a bad mood when you are with your puppy. A puppy is also a lot of work since you want him to grow into a polite and welcomed dog. The sooner you begin the education process, the better. It is always easier to start with a blank slate rather than having to erase unwanted behaviors before you can teach the desired ones. The fifteen chapters you have read provide what you need to get off on the right paw. Here are some highlights I want to make sure you didn't miss.

Chapter 1
So, You Got a Puppy. Now What?

- Dogs are not pack animals that need to be dominated.
- Choose a teaching philosophy that will develop the relation ship you want to have with your dog which is that of teacher/ student.
- Management of unwanted behaviors is as important as teaching wanted behaviors.
- Choose a breed that fits your lifestyle.
- Keep your puppy safe.
- Socialize your puppy while he is young.

Chapter 2
It's Not A Remote Control (Clicker Basics)

- Use a clicker as a behavior marker followed by a reward.
- Learn to follow the rules of using a clicker.
- Practice your timing with the clicker prior to teaching your pup.
- Puppies think like narcissistic lawyers with ADHD.
- Choose rewards carefully.
- Fade out the clicker and reward as each behavior is learned.

Chapter 3
What Was That? (Clicker Conditioning)

- Choose your cookies wisely.
- Power the clicker with the 'Name Game'.

- Puppies don't learn to do it when you say it, if you keep repeating it until they do it.
- Create a release word to end behaviors.
- Teach in several sessions per day enhanced by brief training moments.
- Use alternatives to a mechanical clicker for noise sensitive pups.

Chapter 4
How Do I Teach That? (Teaching Methods)

- Lure, initially, to get what you want.
- Capture behaviors you want repeated.
- Shape behaviors you can't lure or capture.

Chapter 5
No More Accidents ("Toilet" Teaching)

- Peeing inside is not "wrong" to puppies.
- Prevent house training accidents with a crate and supervision.
- Interrupt indoor bathroom accidents.
- Deal with a missed accident with disappointed surprise and a trip outside.
- Your pup asking to go outside is the last piece of the house training puzzle.

Chapter 6
I Can Do Anything (Self-Control For Your Pup)

- Pups should have meals not a buffet.
- Desired behavior starts with the food bowl.
- Teach your pup to leave food on the floor when told.
- Many common foods are toxic to dogs.
- Teach your pup not to grab dropped food.
- Teach 'Find It' as a redirection game.
- Combine 'Find It' and 'Leave It' for an active game with your pup.

Chapter 7
Ouch!!!!!!!!!!!!

- Don't let your pup practice biting your skin or clothing.
- Manage puppy biting prior to teaching replacement behaviors.
- Teach your pup to touch you with his nose.
- Teach your pup to kiss you with his tongue.

Chapter 8
An Open Door Is Not An Invitation

- Teach your pup not to run out of a crate when you open it.
- Teach your pup to wait at the front door whether he is joining you or not.
- Teach your pup to wait before jumping out of the car.

Chapter 9
Easy 'Come'/Easy Go

- Coming to you is the most fun your pup should ever have.
- Coming to you must end with your hand in the collar.
- 'Come' needs to be taught inside for several weeks prior to teaching it outside.
- Distraction is added to the inside 'Come' prior to teaching it outside.
- The consequence for not coming when called is the loss of a great reward.
- The possibility of mechanical failure makes 'Come' a must for every pup.

Chapter 10
Assume Your Position

- Don't make visible food part of the signal for 'Sit'.
- Teach all the body positions you want your pup to know.
- Always release from a body position cue before your pup moves.
- The lure for a body position is the beginning of teaching a hand signal.

Chapter 11
Only Blink, Breathe and Swallow (In Other Words 'Stay')

- 'Stay' is the hardest cue to teach.
- Duration of 'Stay' must be taught before distance.
- 'Stay' should be taught in such small increments that success is always possible.

Chapter 12
World's Most Rhetorical Question: Wanna Go For A Walk?

- Choosing your walking equipment is as important as teaching your dog to walk politely.
- Pulling should be managed until loose leash walking is taught.
- Sniff walks are as important as exercise walks.
- Your dog can walk in front of you, next to you, or behind you as the situation dictates.

Chapter 13
Four on the Floor

- Jumping on people is accidentally reinforced which makes the jumping worse.
- Jumping on furniture should be allowed or not, consistently, even when you are not home.
- Puppies can be kept out of the dishwasher.
- Walking toward a pup pushes him back and walking away draws him toward you.

Chapter 14
Bait and Switch: Dealing With Stealing and Destruction

- Never chase a puppy for a stolen object.
- Trade what's in your puppy's mouth for a cookie.
- Combine 'Trade' with 'Leave It' to discourage stealing.
- Playing 'Tug' is good for your pup when done properly.
- Prevention of destructive behavior is the human's job.

Chapter 15
I Heard You the First Time: Barking Issues

- Puppies need to bark.
- Puppies don't need to bark incessantly.
- Teaching the word 'Quiet' can limit barking.
- Quickly build duration for 'Quiet'.
- Teach your puppy how to be alone, quietly.
- Limit but don't eliminate alarm barking.
- Always listen to and trust your puppy.
- Limit barking outside in the yard.

Enjoy your puppy. He will grow and learn and thrill you beyond all you can imagine. Last week I asked a little girl named Isabella if having a puppy was as good as she thought it would be. She said it all as she responded, "It is even better than I thought it would be. Gibson is amazing. I love to follow him around and watch what he does." This child is well on the road to a wonderful life full of furry delight.   I wish you the same.

For me, my life's wish is that my footprints are always intertwined with those of a dog.

About the Author: Jane has been teaching dogs for competition since 1996 and working with families and their pet dogs since 2004. She is an Associate Certified Dog Behavior Consultant with the International Association of Animal Behavior Consultants (IAABC) and a Canine Good Citizen evaluator for the American Kennel Club. No matter the breed, the age or the situation, kind and gentle teaching, free of pain and fear, are her exclusive methods. To give back to her community, Jane currently offers dog training demonstrations free of charge in her area. These are filmed and shown on Educational Cable Television. Jane lives by this philosophy: *Life, especially that of dogs, is too short for harsh training and too long to be without learning.*

Made in the USA
Middletown, DE
13 March 2015